An Almost English Life

MIRIAM GROSS

An Almost English Life

Published in 2012 by Short Books
3A Exmouth House
Pine Street
EC1R 0JH

10 9 8 7 6 5 4 3 2 1

Poem on page 89, "The Ogre" by WH Auden, reprinted by
permission of Curtis Brown Ltd. Copyright © 1968, renewed.

Photographs of Isaiah Berlin and Lionel Trilling: *Getty Images*

A CIP catalogue record for this book
is available from the British Library.

ISBN 978-1-78072-099-9

Printed and bound by CPI Group (UK) Ltd, Croydon, CR0 4YY

For Tom and Susanna

I

Jerusalem

My mother, though Jewish, was not a 'Jewish mother'. Quite the reverse. She never in her life cooked a meal, as far as I am aware. She was reserved and austere. She disliked all displays of emotion. She often criticised and rarely praised. She was not in the least maternal. I was her only child, but she had wanted a boy, as she often told me – and others in my hearing. In her opinion, most women were frivolous and intellectually inferior. She was a short, slim woman with cropped hair and very good legs. She wore elegant, mannish clothes, and glasses. Despite all this, she seemed to be very popular among her peers and she was attractive to men. How otherwise could she have captured my handsome father? When I was in my twenties she became a high court judge in Germany.

I was born in Jerusalem a year before the outbreak of the Second World War. My parents had met there (my mother was married to someone else at the time), both having left Germany in 1933 soon after Hitler came to power. My mother, who was half Russian and half German, had had to abandon her legal studies in

Berlin when the Nazis decreed that Jews could no longer practise law. My father (who was ten years older) had at that time already built up a successful practice – he had chosen to be a lawyer rather than to work for his family's retail business.

He was exempt from the Nazi ban on Jewish lawyers because he had won an Iron Cross in the First World War. On the other hand, he had defended a social democrat, who had been accused of being a communist, in a high-profile court case: defending 'communists', whether you were Jewish or not, also disbarred you, under Hitler's new rules, from continuing as a lawyer. Not that my father would have stayed in Nazi Germany. Both my parents, like many German Jews who could afford to start a new life, left their families behind and set off for Palestine. They married there in 1937.

Neither of my parents were committed Zionists. On the contrary, my father's wartime experiences as a soldier in the German army had put him off all forms of nationalism. My mother, too, was at that time doubtful about the idea of a Jewish state (before the rise of Hitler, she had been in favour of assimilation, believing that the more Jews and non-Jews intermarried, the more likely it would be that the 'Jewish problem' would gradually fade away). But they wanted to live in a place where Jews were free.

Nor were my parents religious. In common with many German Jews, they did not observe Jewish customs or traditions in any shape or form. Throughout my child-hood I never once entered a synagogue – I barely knew there were such places – and I was brought up in total ignorance even of the most basic tenets of Judaism.

I have often wondered what effect, if any, such a totally secular upbringing has on the development of character. Secular people have never seemed to me less good or kind or honest than believers. But then of course we are all brought up in a Judeo-Christian culture, so there's no way of telling what we would be like without it. Equally, although I've always been aware of a 'God-shaped hole', religious faith of any kind seems to me to be completely irrational and self-deluding. Would I have felt differently if I'd had a religious upbringing? Impossible to know.

My father spoke only German when he arrived in Jerusalem, so a legal career was not open to him. But because he was familiar with the retail business – his family owned a department store in Meiningen, a small town in Thuringia – he decided to set up what was to become the largest women's fashion store in the city. All the installations for the store (he had rented the premises in what was known as the Armenian building: the landlord belonged to Jerusalem's Armenian community) were shipped in from Germany with the help of my father's brother who had remained there, running the family business. This was still possible in the early 1930s. The large glass panes for the shop-front windows were imported from Belgium and apparently caused much trouble by breaking several times.

Our name, May, was carved in stone above the entrance of the shop in three scripts – Roman, Hebrew and Arabic – and the store thrived. Even the queen of

Jordan sometimes came to shop there. So did the emperor Haile Selassie and his entourage, for whom a meal was cooked specially on the premises. Jerusalem was very much smaller in the 1930s and 40s and this large store has now become one of the city's average-sized banks.

Meanwhile, in 1938, when news from Germany became more and more bleak, my father travelled back to his home town to help bring out his brother and his mother. His brother had already been sent to Buchenwald (at that stage known as Ettersberg). He had been warned on the day before Kristallnacht by members of the town's SA (Hitler's 'Brownshirts') – some of whom were husbands or lovers of non-Jews who worked at the store – that something awful would happen during the night.

The perpetrators would not be the local SA but SA members from other areas who did not know the town's Jews personally. He would not be harmed, my uncle was told, if he offered no resistance. All Jewish men (at this stage only men were targeted) would be rounded up, put on lorries and transported to some unknown location. This was exactly what happened. My uncle, dressed in his warmest overcoat – it was a very cold November – was placed on a lorry and taken to the camp. He later gave his coat to the town's elderly rabbi who had also been arrested.

But it was still possible to get people out of the camp if one could afford to pay the considerable sum of 1000 marks. So my father was able to secure my uncle's release. He and my grandmother (my grandfather had died some years previously) sailed on the last ship to leave Germany for Palestine.

My mother, too, went on a journey back to Berlin, to persuade her parents to leave and live with us in Jerusalem. They declined, arguing that things would surely improve and that Germany would soon come to its senses. She never saw them again. Though she didn't talk to me about it, I know she felt that she had not tried hard enough. Many decades later, when my mother was in her nineties, senile and disoriented, she would often suddenly ask, 'But where are my parents?'

In Jerusalem, we lived in a large flat above the shop. My father and his brother ran the business and my mother did the accounts. A succession of cook/house-keepers, usually Arab women (I had had an Arab wet-nurse – breastfeeding was not something my mother could countenance), looked after me in the daytime, though my mother would appear from time to time to ensure that her strict rules were being observed. During mealtimes, for example, I often had to hold books under my arms to make sure that my elbows weren't sticking out. If I didn't finish my spinach at lunchtime, it would be served up again for supper, with a bit of sugar sprinkled on it. The Arab ladies cooked European food.

Before I started school, I spent a great deal of time playing on my own or following the housekeeper around listening to her complaints about my mother. Two other children, sisters who were about the same age as me, lived in our building, but I was not allowed to play with them. They were deemed unsuitable by my mother. She did not consider their Polish family to be sufficiently cultured or respectable. But I remember these two girls, whom I never properly met, more distinctly than many later friends. We used to call to each other, and throw things to one another, across our respective balconies. People often assume that only children are spoilt – and at some level that may be true. But what chiefly impressed me about these sisters was that there were two of them. How lucky that seemed.

Our shop, May – the name rendered in Arabic, Hebrew and Roman script

Not that my childhood in Jerusalem was unhappy. I recall frequent trips to the city's best ice-cream parlour, holidays at the seaside resort of Netanya (now a large town and latterly the site of several Palestinian terrorist attacks, most notably the Passover massacre of 2002), whizzing around the shop on my tricycle, being cosseted by the shop assistants. One of these later married Victor Weisz, the brilliant political cartoonist known as Vicky, who emigrated to England (from Berlin) in 1935.

Best of all, I remember the annual excursion to pick flowers with my adored father. He would take the day off – presumably with the aim of putting in what is now called 'quality time' with me (though I felt that we were covertly conspiring to get away from my mother) – and we would walk hand in hand to the outskirts of Jerusalem. We would clamber across rocky hills looking for the long-stemmed wild cyclamen, pink, purple and white, which sprang up every year in the patches of dusty earth between the rocks. We were always alone on this stony high ground, with its panoramic view of the old city surrounded by olive groves. Even as a small child I could sense that there was something historic and mythical in this landscape, or so it seems to me now.

Apart from our housekeepers and the westernised women who shopped at our store, I didn't meet many Palestinian Arabs. Hostility between Jews and Arabs had considerably increased as more and more refugees from Nazi rule struggled to enter Palestine. After 1939, when the British government decided to limit Jewish immigration, relations between Jews and the British Mandate also deteriorated. I remember many days on which curfews were imposed on the city. I would spend hours leaning out of our window, throwing sweets and chewing gum to the friendly British soldiers patrolling the street below. I very rarely entered the Arab parts of the city, as they were regarded as too dangerous.

One of my most vivid memories, though, is the weekly visit from 'the Arab with the eggs', as we called him. The arrival on our doorstep of this mysterious figure never failed to thrill and terrify me. There he would stand, wrapped from head to toe in layers of what looked like grey blankets, his swarthy face barely visible beneath his Arab headdress. He would reach deep into the folds of his garments, fumbling around in the area of his chest until, at last, he would pull out an egg – covered in bits of straw. Sometimes he produced two eggs. Eggs were a rare luxury in those wartime years, and he would charge for them accordingly.

I spent three unremarkable years at a school in Jerusalem. The children mostly came from the same kind of immigrant families as I did, though there were some who had lived in the city for generations. I made many friends and was even allowed to bring some of them home. Nearly every day when I came back from school my mother would insist that, when I'd finished my homework, I spent a further hour learning to read and write in German, using the Roman alphabet (as opposed to the Hebrew script taught at school). This seemed to me tyrannical, but it was to make my life much easier later.

I don't think my father had much say in my upbringing. Or if he did, he was overruled. The contrast between my parents' characters could hardly have been greater. My father was at all times good-humoured and tolerant – I never heard him say a cross or unkind word. Nor did he ever complain about anything. He inspired the loyalty of everyone who had dealings with him. Meanwhile, he put up with my mother's criticism and disparagement with saintly patience.

My parents were never very happy in Palestine. They did not succeed in learning to speak Hebrew fluently, they didn't like the heat, and both of them, particularly my father, wanted to resume their legal careers. Above all, they deeply disapproved of the terrorist tactics some Jewish underground organisations had been deploying against the British since the end of the war. The bombing of the King David Hotel – site of the British Mandate's military headquarters and central offices – in July 1946 was a turning point. As it happened, this imposing grand hotel had been one of the highlights of my parents' social life – they went dancing there once a week.

My father and me in Jerusalem, 1945

I had no idea, when we set sail for Europe in 1947 (I was nearly nine), that I was never to return – or at least not for more than 30 years, and then as a tourist. Presumably my parents thought that to explain that we were emigrating would upset me too much; or perhaps they feared that I would cause trouble. In any event, I was not given the chance to say goodbye to my school friends or to anyone else.

After a brief holiday in Switzerland, my parents travelled on to America and to England to look for work and to decide where they wanted to settle. Meanwhile, they deposited me at a small Swiss boarding school where I was overwhelmed by so many new impressions and demands that I soon began to forget my old life. I also began to forget the Hebrew language.

Much, perhaps too much, has been said and written about the importance of 'roots'. Does being uprooted from the country in which you were born and where you spent half your childhood leave some indefinable emotional scar? I don't believe so. In any case, it has been a commonplace occurrence ever since the beginning of the twentieth century. I did, however, have a surprising experience when I went to see the Hollywood epic *Exodus*, sometime in my thirties. Before this very mediocre film begins, while the credits are rolling, the wide screen is filled with some beautiful panoramic scenes of Jerusalem and its surrounding hills and olive trees. As soon as I saw this, I unexpectedly burst into tears.

Back to Jerusalem – I

I didn't go back to Jerusalem for about 30 years, mainly because I was too busy – getting married, having children, working, going on holidays to less dangerous places. But

I have been back for three or four short visits, of which the first and last are the most memorable. Naturally, on my first visit after an absence of so long, I immediately set off from my hotel to look for the street and the house in which I had spent my early childhood. Though Jerusalem had expanded enormously, the part of it in which we had lived, now rather down at heel, was largely unchanged. I found the street (Princess Mary Avenue under the British Mandate, now Shlomzion Hamalka Street) easily enough and I recognised the look and feel of it, even if not the details of its topography.

What was much harder to find, because of the tricks that memory plays, was the actual house. I was absolutely certain that our shop – now converted, I had been told, into a bank – and the flat above it which had been my home, was on the right-hand side of the street. But there was no sign of a bank. So I went into shop after shop – ironmongers', chemists', grocers' – asking assistants whether there was a large bank anywhere in the vicinity. They all pointed to the other side of the road, but I was convinced that couldn't be it.

When I came to the end of the street, I retraced my steps and asked them all again whether by any chance they remembered, or knew of, a large fashion store called May which had once existed somewhere nearby. They'd never heard of it. I was on the point of giving up in despair when one of the assistants suggested that I should ask the owner of the small bookshop opposite – he had been around for donkey's years.

So I crossed the road, went through an unobtrusive

doorway and found myself in semi-darkness. When my eyes adjusted to the dim light, I realised that I had stepped backwards in time, into a cramped, dusty, Dickensian cave in which every corner and crevice was jammed with books. Floor-to-ceiling shelves on both sides of a long, narrow room were filled to overflowing, and stacks of books of every size and shape were piled high on the floor. At first I thought that there was no one in this book-paradise. But as I moved further into it, I saw a light at the back of the room; and then I discerned a stooped figure sitting at a desk. It was a very old man – he must have been well into his eighties – bent over some manuscripts.

I advanced cautiously. 'Sorry to disturb you, but I wonder whether you can help me. I am looking for the house in which, many years ago, there was a fashion shop – May.' As soon as he heard the name the man leaped from his chair, waving his arms about. 'May was here, in this building! Come, I'll show you.' He ran, stumbling ahead of me back into the street. 'Here,' he pointed to the bank. 'This was May.'

Of course – it all fell into place. How disoriented I had been. The three large glass shop windows were still there and the flat above looked instantly familiar. 'I was born here,' I told him, 'my name used to be May.' The old man looked at me and smiled. 'You must be the daughter of Kurt May. I knew him very well. He helped me get this shop in 1935. And he helped me later, too.' Tears started streaming down his face – as they did down mine. I could hardly speak. We stood there for a while and then

I thanked him, we shook hands and he disappeared back among his books.

Later I learned that his name was Ludwig Mayer, that he had come to Jerusalem from Berlin in 1908, that he was an internationally renowned bookseller and that his shop was known as 'Israel's first quality bookshop'. It was regarded as a landmark of Zionist history. I have always regretted that I didn't go back and talk to him further. There are so many questions I would like to have asked him. At the time, though, I thought that he was too busy and wouldn't want to be disturbed again. I doubt that I was right about that.

II

England – via Switzerland

After leaving Palestine (as it still was in 1947), I spent almost a year, including holidays, at a Swiss-German-speaking boarding school in Celerina, a small village in the Engadine. Only a few things from this time stick in my mind. One is the way packages were instantly confiscated. Every month my parents would send a parcel of sweets from America (sweets were still in short supply all over post-war Europe, even in chocolate-fixated Switzerland). This was opened by the school's headmistress and its contents locked away in a cupboard. Once a week, on Wednesdays, the cupboard would be opened and the sweets equally distributed in tiny portions among all the pupils. Needless to say, I found this very distressing.

Another memory is being told the facts of life by a Russian girl called Ludmilla. She was known as a bit of a fantasist, so I didn't for a moment believe the disgusting proceedings she described to me. Still, it must have made an impact, otherwise why do I remember the occasion so clearly? We were sitting on a garden swing at the time. I also recall being overwhelmed by the power of Schiller's poetic drama *Don Carlos*, brilliantly read aloud by the literature teacher. And I certainly haven't forgotten how, when my parents finally came back, after such a long absence, I wasn't allowed to see them because they arrived at the school after bedtime. Even though I could hear their voices downstairs, I had to wait till the next day.

Meanwhile, my father had been offered an important and very suitable job. The United Restitution Organisation (URO), an Anglo-American legal aid society to assist and compensate the victims of Nazi persecution, was set up in 1948. Initially, it was planned as a five-year project. But in the course of the next decade it grew into a world-wide enterprise, with offices in nineteen countries and 1000 staff. Over the years it assisted and recompensed more than 200,000 people, mainly Jews but also gypsies and others. My father, who became its director-general in 1955, ended up working for the URO for 40 years, until the age of 91. 'There are literally hundreds of thousands of people who may never have heard the name of Kurt May,' said his obituary in the *Independent*, 'but who are heavily in his debt. He conducted his work with a passion for justice, an unshakable belief in the right to demand the redress for wrongs and always maintained the greatest degree of dignity in the pursuit of this cause.'

There was, however, a downside to this job: the URO's central offices were in Frankfurt and, understandably, the last thing my parents had intended was to return to Germany. But they reluctantly agreed to go back in 1948, partly because of what they thought was the temporary nature of the job, and partly because they would live there among Americans – as part of the post-war American occupation of southern Germany.

What they couldn't accept, though, was that I should be brought up and educated as a German. My mother had already visited England to search for a suitable boarding school for me. At that time, the kind of girls' schools she looked at – Roedean and Cheltenham Ladies' College – did not accept pupils like me who spoke no English. So she opted for Dartington Hall, the co-educational, experimental school in south Devon based on the 'progressive' ideas of the American philosopher John Dewey.

Dartington Hall School

My mother was not a great believer in the unstructured approach to education or in the 'laissez-faire' attitude to learning which were Dartington's guiding principles. But she liked the school's teachers, and its setting – as well she might. The teachers were for the most part ideal-istic and interesting individuals, some of whom had, for one reason or another, opted out of conventional society; quite a number were refugees from Nazi Europe or Franco's Spain. The setting was the beautiful 1000-acre estate, with its grand medieval hall, which had been bought in 1925 by a philanthropic couple, the Elmhirsts – a Yorkshireman and an American heiress. One of their objectives was to build a school in which children would be free from the constraints and restrictions of the educational system which prevailed at the time.

I was just ten when my mother escorted me to the 'Middle School' – a set of ultra-modern Bauhaus-style buildings which housed children aged from six to thirteen – and left me there to sink or swim.

I sank, temporarily at least. Most children at that age are not particularly kind when someone who can't speak their language and doesn't know how to play their games or join in their routines is placed in their midst. Even when they are kind, it is a miserable experience to be completely cut off, without a single family member or trusted friend in the whole country to speak to or confide in. Every evening I used to hide in a corner of the school's large, dark gym so that I could cry without being seen. My mother would occasionally phone from Germany – a very difficult procedure in the late 1940s – and I would beg her to come and take me away. She always told me to hold on a little longer because things were bound to get better. Finally she promised to fetch me if I was still unhappy after six months. When this longed-for day arrived, my mother broke her promise. She didn't come – and I never really forgave her.

Looking back now, as a mother myself, it is incomprehensible to me how any parent could abandon a child in this way – unless there is absolutely no other choice. It's true that the perception of both childhood and parenthood in Western societies has greatly changed over the past 60 years. At that time it was regarded as normal, for parents who could afford the fees, to send their children away for weeks on end at the age of eight. Innumerable memoirs of unhappy childhoods attest to this. Since

then we have become much more sensitive to the vulner-
abilities and needs of children and to the importance of
parental support. Nevertheless, I think my total isola-
tion, first in Switzerland and immediately afterwards in
England, was unusually hard-hearted even for those days.
But then my parents were faced with a cruel dilemma,
created by Hitler and anti-Semitism.

My mother, Vera: she was usually right

As it turned out, my mother had been right. Not long
afterwards, I began to speak English fluently, I made
friends and became an integrated member of the school.
Occasionally my parents came to visit me, but my chief
memory of these occasions is the embarrassment I felt
because of their German accents. For the next eight years
I was very happy at Dartington. So much so that, during
the holidays, which I usually spent in Frankfurt where I
had no friends, I used to wait feverishly for the beginning
of the next term. As my parents had hoped, I had become
thoroughly anglicised.

Love-objects

All my life I have been in the grip of an infatuation – or had a 'crush', or been in love – with someone or other. Whether being continuously 'in love' is a genetic condition, or whether it is the result of insufficient closeness and support during childhood, I have no idea. Whatever the reason, there were very few periods in my life (until I married my present husband at the age of 55) when I wasn't pining for, or agonising about, or impatiently anticipating, a meeting with a loved one – usually male but, while at school, also female and, on one occasion, a dog. My first romantic attachment occurred when I was nine, while on vacation with my parents at a Swiss hotel, just after my year there at boarding school and before first coming to England. Also staying at the hotel was a Swedish family whose son, a dark-haired boy, was a year or two older than me. We became inseparable companions for two or three weeks. At the end of the holiday, of course, we had to separate and I was heartbroken.

This is a commonplace childhood experience and I would probably have forgotten all about it; but it has stuck in my mind because it was the first time, as far as I remember, that my stern mother displayed an unexpected softer side. On the evening of the boy's departure, when she came into my bedroom to say goodnight, she found me weeping into my pillow. She sat on my bed and stroked my hair, 'Poor child, you will have many more such painful partings,' my mother said; or words to that effect.

My love affair with a dog took place a few months

later. My mother and I were living in a rented one-bedroom flat in a quiet street in London's West Hampstead during one of my first English school holidays. One morning, a sprightly fox terrier inexplicably appeared in the small front garden. There were no owners in sight, but the dog was by no means a stray. His name and address were embossed on an elegant dog collar: Caesar, from Frognal, a much more fashionable part of Hampstead – about half a mile away – than the one he now found himself in. (We were often to walk there together and always found his home, an imposing ultra-modern building, deserted; presumably his owners were at work.)

The arrival of this intelligent dog was a godsend, since at that time I had not yet made any English friends. Caesar soon followed me out of the gate and trotted along beside me all the way to Hampstead Heath and all the way back again. On our return I gave him some water and from that day we spent all our waking hours together. He would turn up at the front door every morning at 6am, and he would leave again at bedtime. I can't now remember what we did exactly – run around playing with sticks and balls, I suppose. When my mother wanted me to accompany her on a shopping trip, or on any other outing, I would throw a hysterical fit and sulk until we got back home and I was reunited with my canine soulmate, who would be faithfully waiting near the front door. Caesar very rarely entered our flat. My mother was no animal lover and, looking back now, I realise that she must have tolerated the situation because it kept me harmlessly and happily out of the way from dawn till dusk.

My passion for Caesar fizzled out when I went back to school and I never saw him again, though I always looked around for him while walking in the streets of Hampstead. But ever since this episode, I have been convinced that the loyalty of dogs is not just directed at the person who provides their food (Caesar received his main meal at his own home, in the evenings) or at the person whom they regard – because of an inbred sense of social hierarchy – as the leader of their pack. Caesar, I'm sure, loved me for myself, as I did him.

No rewards for effort

Dartington Hall, which was one of the handful of experimental schools founded before the Second World War, took a very different view of how children should learn and how teachers should teach from that commonly held at the time. At Dartington, education was not about one person who knows more than another passing on that knowledge; rather, it was a process that allowed children to discover things for themselves, albeit with guidance from teachers. Pupils were not expected to memorise facts or learn anything by rote. They were encouraged to follow their own interests in their own way and at their own pace.

These educational ideals were still regarded by most people as, at best, absurdly utopian or, at worst, hopelessly cranky. Later, in the 60s, many of them were adopted, with disastrous results, in state schools throughout England.

We in the 'Middle School' were too young to understand this educational philosophy and, luckily, many of the teachers did not seem fully to believe in it. The maths teacher, for example, an elderly lady whose grey hair was tied back in an old-fashioned bun, made us memorise our multiplication tables with the aid of 'Smarties tests'. We would be awarded prizes of these much-coveted little multi-coloured chocolates if we did well. This method worked brilliantly (particularly as sweets were still rationed in this post-war period) and I have remembered my times-tables ever since – but it didn't exactly chime with the school's anti-rote-learning or anti-competitive ethos.

On the whole, classes were very informal – we called teachers by their first names or by nicknames – and we enjoyed a huge amount of freedom, and free time, compared with children in most schools. In other ways, too, we were extraordinarily privileged. Dartington was one of the very few schools, for example, where every child had his or her own bedroom. Uniforms were, of course, spurned. We wore casual 'weekend' clothes – jeans had not yet become a unisex uniform.

It took about a year for my English to become fluent – I remember the surprise, at around this time, expressed by the father of a friend, on hearing that I wasn't English – and my school life gradually began to look up. Luckily for me, there was a terrific craze for roller-skating a year or so after I arrived, and because I had learned ice-skating in Switzerland, I was a whizz at this 'sport'. So my lowly status was considerably enhanced.

Indeed it wasn't long before I became one of the more disruptive members of my class. I remember, for instance, eagerly throwing myself into a cruel campaign to make life intolerable for the English teacher. We had somehow decided that this extremely pleasant young man – and excellent teacher – had bad breath. So we not only passed him notes during lessons complaining about his affliction, we also sent warnings about it to his girlfriend, who worked in another part of the school. I recall cutting out what was at the time a famous advertisement for Colgate toothpaste and sticking it to his desk. The ad showed a toothily smiling face, its mouth surrounded by a kind of sparkly halo; the accompanying slogan promised to endow users with the 'Colgate ring of confidence'. We thought this hilarious. The hapless teacher, who went on to become one of the bosses of BBC Radio 3 music, later married the young woman, despite our best efforts.

Most of my memories of this time involve out-of-class activities. I particularly recall sitting around for hours, convulsed in giggles, while an elder girl read aloud from a sex manual which she had managed to obtain. We (girls) also spent a lot of time practising 'French kissing', which we had witnessed in the cinema. We did this while walking around the school grounds.

In those pre-television days, going to see a film was an intensely thrilling treat. The nearest cinema was to be found in the seaside town of Paignton where, about twice a term, one of the teachers would take us by bus to see the latest 'U' (universal, i.e. for all ages) certificate film. The programme would usually include two films, one of them a B movie. These shorter, low-budget productions – mostly crime stories – which were wonderfully free from 'art-house', or any other pretensions, were more lurid and therefore often more gripping than the main feature.

Like all girls in their early teens, we hero-worshipped the stars of the day – Tony Curtis, Gary Cooper, Rock Hudson, Ava Gardner, Elizabeth Taylor. (Many years later, at a smart London party, I spent some time politely talking to a stocky middle-aged woman, all the while wondering how I could make my getaway and meet some of the more glamorous people in the room. It was only when another guest joined us that I discovered I'd been talking to Ava Gardner.)

On free afternoons, we would often walk to the beautiful gardens adjoining the great medieval hall. There an open-air theatre had been created, surrounded by immaculately groomed hedges. At its edge stood a large stone statue of a reclining woman, known as Big Bottom Bertha. She had a tiny bullet head and huge hind quarters, and was unmistakeably the work of the sculptor Henry Moore. We would spend many hilarious hours climbing around on this curvaceous figure and re-enacting some of the love scenes we'd witnessed on screen. 'Take me, I am yours', 'I crave your tender touch,' we would wail. This activity took place exclusively among girls. Boys, as is well known, are much smaller and less developed in their early teens than girls. Indeed, I can't say that a single boy made the slightest impression on me during these years.

One of my more painful recollections of this period stemmed precisely from the fact that I was one of the tallest children in my year. The music teacher had conceived an ambitious plan: to stage an opera, with piano, rather than an orchestral, accompaniment – Verdi's *Il Trovatore*. On the basis of my height, rather than my singing voice, she decided that I should be cast in the title role, that of Manrico, the troubadour. This was all very exciting, and when we started rehearsing things didn't go too badly. It was obvious that my voice didn't carry very far and that the girls playing the other main parts – Manrico's old mother and his young inamorata – were much better singers as well as much better actors than I was. But my efforts were passable.

Not so on the big night. During the actual performance (which many parents, though thankfully not mine, had travelled to Devon to attend), I failed to reach a single high note in any of my songs; and, much worse, in the scene where Manrico is off-stage, heard but not seen – he is incarcerated in a nearby prison, singing his heart out – the audience, so I was later told, could hear nothing at all.

After the show, various teachers came backstage to congratulate the cast. They all, rightly, lavished praise on my co-protagonists. To me they tactfully said nothing. Except for one teacher who, attempting to be kind, remarked, 'You looked very nice, Miriam.' I knew, of course, that this meant 'You were hopeless.'

Because the school was part of a large, 'utopian' community (there was, for example, a music school for adults at the actual hall), it attracted many artistic people and was renowned for its teaching of arts and crafts. We had a wide range of opportunities: we could learn all kinds of musical instruments; we could paint in many mediums in a well-equipped art room; we could be taught how to make clay pots and figurines by a professional potter in a studio complete with potter's wheel and kiln.

I embarked on several artistic activities with great enthusiasm – but I never advanced very far. As soon as I reached the stage when a bit more effort and concentration were required, I quickly lost heart. For example, I made great strides at the piano, learning quite intricate pieces off by heart; but when it became impossible to make further progress without learning to sight-read, I soon stopped going to lessons. The same happened with my attempts at pottery. At first I produced some quaint vases and ashtrays. Then, when I began to realise that making proper pots, just like becoming a proficient piano player, required a great deal of practice, I gave up on this challenging activity altogether.

I don't blame myself for these failures. I blame the school, with its misconceived notion that young pupils should be given lots of choices and should never be pressurised into doing anything unless they felt like it. Only the rarest of children, given the options of practising scales or playing with their friends, will choose to practise. At Dartington, there were no rewards for effort in any subject, artistic or otherwise; nor were there penalties for idleness. As a result, at this stage of our education, we learned very little.

What a waste of our potential. It is during these early years that children have better memories than they will ever have again – for absorbing basic historical facts and dates, for example, or for learning poems by heart. And it is at this stage that habits of concentration and application are instilled. People argue that you can always catch up later and that 'happiness' is more important in childhood than knowledge. This seems nonsense to me. Children are eager for information and enjoy knowing things by heart – indeed, knowledge is one of the more reliable routes to happiness. But it can't be acquired in the 'do-it-yourself' atmosphere which pertained at Dartington. I can't speak for others, but at the age of thirteen, when we moved to the Senior School, my 'memory bank' was pretty much empty.

These thoughts did not, of course, occur to me at the time, though they certainly did in my later teens when I found that I had no basic framework into which to fit the new things that I was learning.

A small, self-contained democratic republic

The first thing I remember about my new life at the Senior School is a ping-pong game. The Senior School was located in a different, equally beautiful, part of the Dartington estate, surrounded by fields and woodlands. It was housed in a large, rectangular building that had been brilliantly designed to fulfil the requirements of a boarding school. At its centre there was a spacious rectangular courtyard – the hub of school life. This was flanked on two sides by our individual bedrooms (girls and boys were mixed together), while the other two sides were given over to classrooms and other communal spaces. Soon after our arrival, my friend Theodora (known as Theo) – who had performed so well in the role of the mother in *Il Trovatore* – and I were exploring our new environment when we chanced upon a room containing a ping-pong table. I had occasionally played ping-pong in hotels with my father, and Theo also knew how to play, so we started a game.

Just as we were getting going and finding that we could manage quite long rallies, a group of older boys – they must have been sixteen or seventeen – rowdily burst into the room, in the hope of having a game themselves. We were aghast. In their eyes we must have been total pipsqueaks – the lowliest form of school life. Looking back, I'm surprised we didn't immediately throw down our bats and flee. However, we carried on with our game, and soon the boys started excitedly taking sides, some of them backing Theo, others egging me on. Not that they knew our names; they differentiated between us by our height – I was the slightly taller one. It turned into an unexpectedly exhilarating and long-drawn-out contest, with much cheering and clapping.

This table tennis incident, absurd though it may seem, felt like a turning point in my school life. Before it, I had always thought of myself as a shadowy bit-player, a tolerated hanger-on. Post-ping-pong, I suddenly moved much nearer to centre stage. I don't think Theo experienced the event in the same way; she was already a much more self-confident person, less shy, and probably less vain. In any event, my morale, as well as my standing, received a great boost. A year or so later, one of these bigwig ping-pong spectators started paying court to me. He became my first boyfriend.

Pupils at the Senior School were treated, as far as possible, like adults – adults inhabiting a small, self-contained democratic republic. There weren't many rules, but those that existed were mostly made at a weekly meeting, a kind of mini-parliament, known as 'Moot'. Everyone could attend and anyone could contribute. Like everything at the school, Moot meetings were informal, with most attendees sitting – often sprawling – on the floor, while various motions were discussed and debated. When all the arguments had been put, a vote would be taken. The rules arrived at in this way were on the whole sensible and public-spirited – establishing fairly early bedtimes for example, or requiring that everyone do their share of unpleasant chores. Much later, in our A-level days, a friend (Hilary Dickinson) and I wrote a satirical poem about Moot for the school magazine. Its opening lines were:

Thursday after lunch and the room is full,
How eager they all are to govern their school.

Its theme was a motion put forward by some girls who wanted to change the rules about how to obtain second helpings of food:

The girls to queue are much too shy
In case they catch their boyfriend's eye

Whether this was a real-life motion or whether we'd invented it, I now can't recall.

Moot meetings were presided over with great incisiveness by our distinguished headmaster W.B. Curry (known as Curry), an acknowledged authority on progressive education, a pacifist and the author of several highly praised books, among them *Education for Sanity*. Curry, who was headmaster from 1931 to 1957 – throughout my time at the school – was a short, round, bald man with, it seemed to me, a startlingly wizened face. Later, I discovered to my astonishment that he was a non-stop, and often successful, womaniser.

I attended Moot meetings regularly, especially in my later teens, but as far as I remember I never uttered a single word at any of them. This was not because I had nothing to say; it was because I was paralysed by shyness, and fear. Whenever I wanted to make a point, my heart would start pounding while I waited for the right moment; then, when the moment came, I simply didn't dare open my mouth. This terror of public speaking has afflicted me throughout my life. How is it that some people, my friend Theo, for example, can speak in public in exactly the same normal way as they speak in private, while I – an opinionated and assertive person in private – am frozen with fright in public? There are, no doubt, various psychological explanations. But I think that this condition, from which quite a number of people, mainly women, seem to suffer, could have been cured if we had been made to practise public speaking in the course of school lessons or debating societies.

Making people do things, however, went against all of Dartington's educational principles. The school's policy was to trust its pupils to adopt a sensible and conscientious attitude to their studies, as well as to their extra-curricular activities. We were expected and encouraged by the teachers to go to lessons and to participate in school sports, but there were no punishments or sanctions if we didn't. Similarly we were counted on to abstain from anti-social behaviour. Most children, if trusted to behave responsibly, will repay this trust. We did go to lessons, we did play school games, we did perform our share of tedious tasks, and we did behave with consideration to others. It was a social contract that worked.

Whether it would have worked in a larger, less well-endowed school (the Senior School contained about 100 pupils), where the children came from less privileged backgrounds, is difficult to say. I rather doubt it. But at Dartington the atmosphere was one of easy tolerance and equality. There was very little prejudice of any kind, almost no snobbery, hardly any cliquishness and not much bullying. Nearly all the children, including me, were unusually stress-free and happy.

Nevertheless, there was something wrong with this form of education, at any rate as far as I was concerned. The absence of grades for school work, the disapproval of competition, the distaste for ambition, the disdain for structure and discipline, the unlimited freedoms – all these 'progressive' ideals resulted in a sapping of our energy. We were too relaxed, too laid-back. A faint aura of lethargy hung over the place. Nobody put much effort, or many hours, into academic work – at least not until the pressure of national exams started to loom.

The alternative pastimes – gossiping, flirting, discussing each other's personalities, lolling around looking at magazines – were too tempting to resist. I recall one day sitting in the school library – I don't think anyone else was in it – researching a history project. What a pity, I remember thinking to myself, that I don't have more time for this fascinating and absorbing activity; if I stay in the library much longer I might miss out on chatting with my friends, or walking to the nearest tuck shop to buy sweets, or hearing some important new development in one of the many romantic relationships being conducted at the time, possibly even my own. So naturally I abandoned my researches and left the library. But this idle way of life troubled me even then – the Protestant work ethic (by no means the exclusive preserve of Protestants), must have been instilled in me at a very early age. Or, more likely, there is a gene for it.

The subject I most enjoyed when we first arrived at the Senior School was Latin. This may have had something to do with the Latin teacher, a sweet, kind, elderly man, who was a refugee from Nazi Germany. He was known as Rosie – short for Rosenberg. Rosie was an old-fashioned teacher – he had to be: you can't teach first-year Latin – *amo, amas, amat* – without throwing in a bit of non-progressive rote-learning. (This may be one reason why Latin was dropped by most state schools when they adopted progressive education.) Because of our similar backgrounds, or maybe simply because he had a German accent like my parents, I felt that there was a special rapport between Rosie and me.

At that time, I only had the vaguest awareness of the Holocaust and of anti-Semitism. My parents, wishing to protect me from the knowledge of human evil, had, as far as I remember, never mentioned it; nor had anyone at school. So I knew nothing of Rosie's story. But he must have known something of mine, and perhaps my feeling of affinity with him stemmed from what I sensed was a heightened interest in my doings, a covert attentiveness towards me in Latin lessons. We could have talked to each other in German, but we never did. A shadow, at that time, hung over the language.

Sadly, Rosie died soon after we took our O-level exams. There was very little demand at the school for Latin, and no-one was appointed to replace him. So when I, and one other pupil, decided that we wanted to take A-level Latin, the headmaster conceived the idea of summoning the Latin master from Totnes grammar school once a week to instruct the two of us in the splendours of Virgil, Horace and Tacitus. This scheme worked brilliantly. I can't remember the man's name, but I remember what he looked like: tall, bony, dark and dour. And he was a formidable teacher. It was my first and only experience of rigorous, exacting teaching. Not to have done every scrap of one's homework would have been unthinkable. I thoroughly enjoyed two years of this stimulating grammar-school approach.

During the first few years at the senior school, though, my two main preoccupations, in common with most teenage girls – and many boys too – were music and affairs of the heart. These two realms of experience are, of course, intimately connected. The music about which I became passionate, believing it to be superior to any other form, was traditional Dixieland jazz. I was introduced to it soon after the pivotal ping-pong game, when I became part of a small group of students, most of them slightly older, who were connoisseurs of this marvellous genre.

Dartington cartoon, by Mark Boxer

We would spend long afternoons sitting in the cramped bedroom of someone who owned a gramophone, and listen, enraptured, to melody after melody – some plangent, some joyful – created by the black musicians of the American South in the early decades of the twentieth century. I can now only remember some of the better-known names – Louis Armstrong, Johnny Dodds, Kid Ory, Jelly Roll Morton, Bessie Smith, Bunk Johnson, Sidney Bechet – but at the time I could identify dozens of players or singers as soon as I heard their first notes. Some of my fellow jazz fans had formed a band of their own in which I occasionally played the drums; it would perform 'jam sessions' in the school's large assembly hall.

So addicted was I to this music that during the holidays, which I mostly spent with my parents in their flat in Frankfurt (at that time still part of the American occupied zone), I would endlessly listen to all manner of radio shows on the American Forces Network in the hope that a piece of jazz might suddenly be included. This did occasionally happen. If my parents inadvertently talked to me during one of these precious moments, I would fly into a rage. They, of course, regarded jazz as a form of caterwauling non-music, and I regarded them as hopeless philistines. But they showed great forbearance and eventually even gave me a gramophone. Naturally, I spent all my pocket money on jazz records. Many years later I took a huge pile of these obsolete 78s to a charity shop.

But it was not only the strains of New Orleans blues that wafted back and forth across the Senior School campus. The air was also thick with our infatuations – requited and unrequited. I must have been about fourteen when, to my surprise (and, I think, that of others), two of the school's most senior boys – they were doing their A-levels at the time – became rivals for my affections. This, for me, was heady stuff and I spent rather too long stringing them both along. Not that I didn't know which one I 'loved' – I knew perfectly well (one of the ping-pong spectators); but I was reluctant to relinquish the other one, who was perhaps the more intellectual of the two. He used to write me long letters, one of which complained that I 'turned him on and off like a tap'. This struck me at the time as a brilliant metaphor, indicating a great future writer. (Tragically, this boy, Niall, the son of the Irish playwright Sean O'Casey, died of leukaemia a few years after leaving school.)

However, I did finally declare my commitment to the other boy. He was one of the school's football stars, an accomplished jazz trumpeter and an excellent ballroom dancer. We embarked on what became a truly romantic relationship, pledging eternal love and future marriage. It lasted until he left the school to go to university.

It was part of the school's unwritten constitution that sexual intercourse was out of bounds. We went in for a great deal of kissing and smooching and even lying on beds together, but we were trusted not to 'go all the way', and, as far as I know, no one did. However, we spent many hours of each day either seeing our boy/girlfriends or, when not actually seeing them, talking about them, or when not talking about them, talking about someone else's romance. This goes on in all schools to some extent, especially in schools where there are girls – teenage girls, as is well known, tending to be more interested in emotional matters than boys. But it would have been impossible, within a traditional educational system, to devote as much time to relationships as we did.

Matters of the heart are, of course, the stuff of most great art – literature, opera, drama and so on – and it could be argued that discussing them, analysing them, speculating about them, is an important part of the learning experience. There is certainly some truth in this, within limits. But at Dartington there were no limits to our freedom to lounge around gossiping. Since we had no external incentives to study, most of us naturally preferred to attend to the urgent concerns of our own and our friends' private lives than to focus on such matters as the pros and cons of the 1832 Reform Bill. Yet learning about the Reform Bill – which one is unlikely ever again to have an opportunity of doing – provides insights into politics that may prove very valuable in later life. Studying one's emotional life, on the other hand, can be done outside school hours.

I have never quite forgiven Dartington for allowing me to waste so much valuable time – for not spurring me on to learn more. For example, I didn't even try to attend classes in physics or chemistry, which at that time were still regarded mainly as 'boys' subjects'; I gave up on biology because I found it too demanding; and after being asked to leave a geography lesson for disruptive behaviour, I dropped the subject altogether. It's true that

I was extremely lazy – but so are most teenagers.

Treating schoolchildren like adults is all very well in some respects, but when it comes to school work, it is utterly wrong-headed. Most children, and quite a few adults too, need sticks and carrots. It was not until the pressure of O- and A-level exams forced me to concentrate that I discovered that Noel Coward had a point: 'Work is more fun than fun.'

Ballroom dancing and nude bathing

Not that we didn't have fun at Dartington. One of the greatest sources of enjoyment, as far as I was concerned, was ballroom dancing. Once a week, a tall, burly, jovial man who worked somewhere on the estate would arrive in formal jacket and tie and teach us proper dance steps. He had a very straight back, I recall, and his bottom stuck out slightly while dancing (as many people's do). Foxtrots, quicksteps, waltzes, polkas, even tangos were all part of his repertory. He would have a twirl with each of us in turn, demonstrating how to hold or be held by your partner and how to move in unison. We would practise 'slow-quick-quick-slow' to the records of Victor Sylvester, one of the most popular dance bands of the day. Even more fun was dancing, or rather jiving, to the school's live jazz band when they held 'sessions' on Saturday evenings.

All this now seems impossibly old-fashioned. But I have been convinced ever since that, for many people, dancing – however inexpert or self-taught – is one of the most therapeutic activities on earth and one of the most effective ways of achieving happiness, even if only temporary. Unfortunately, there isn't nearly enough social dancing in 21st-century England, not at any rate in the circles in which I move. And most schools seem to have dropped it years ago.

But the activity for which Dartington was best known, or perhaps most notorious, was nude, mixed bathing. The Senior School had a swimming pool – about two minutes' walk away from the main building – at which swimming naked was the order of the day. Teachers as well as pupils – or anyone of any age who wished to use the pool – were expected to take off all their clothes, leave them lying on a grassy bank and avail themselves of this liberating experience.

I have no idea how this custom originated – probably with the headmaster W.B. Curry, who, in his book *The School*, wrote: 'It is desirable for boys and girls to see each other wholly or partially undressed as, so to speak, part of the day's work, and without having to make any special effort to do so. In this way the furtive curiosity from which so many adolescents suffer is greatly diminished... I think it is almost certain that, in children at least, nudity after the first few occasions, diminishes rather than increases sexual interest.'

This is undoubtedly true. The area around our swimming pool was a singularly unsexy place. Boys who might climb up a drainpipe at the school itself in order to catch a glimpse of a girl having a bath, would show not the slightest interest in the same girl's nude body (often

Nude bathing at Dartington – an integral part of the
school's enlightened ethos

goose-pimply from the cold) as she made her way into
the chilly water.

I can't now recall what I felt about swimming naked
in the first year or two of Senior School, when I was thirteen and fourteen; I probably went along with it quite
happily. But I do know that, as I grew older, I found it
more and more embarrassing. I didn't dare admit this to
anyone – and hardly to myself – for a very long time.
Nude bathing was such an integral part of the school's
enlightened ethos that to question it would have been
regarded as deeply regressive and bourgeois – the equivalent of objecting to, say, gender equality today. But truth
will out, and we older girls finally, and guiltily, started
confessing to each other that we felt extremely inhibited
about being seen without our clothes on. We had no

wish to expose our wobbly bits to all and sundry. If only we could wear bathing suits, we all agreed, we would go swimming much more often. I suspect most of the boys felt much the same way, though of course I never talked about this uncomfortable subject to any male.

There was one boy who swam against the tide, so to speak, and always wore swimming trunks. Naturally, we all thought there was something fundamentally wrong either with his body, or with his mind, or both. Looking back on it now, it strikes me that he showed exceptional moral courage, or sang-froid – certainly more than we older girls did. None of us even had the nerve to bring up the topic at Moot meetings, or actually to propose a motion we had drafted, to make bathing suits acceptable. So we continued to bathe naked, but more and more self-consciously, and less and less frequently. (After Curry's departure as headmaster in 1957, nudity became optional.)

A little learning

But such matters shouldn't detract from Dartington's real strengths. There were some excellent teachers at the school, particularly in my two main subjects, English and history. I don't suppose that their teaching differed much from that of good teachers in non-progressive schools. They focused on teaching us to think for ourselves, to look at all sides of a question, not to accept anything at face value, to check everything we said or read against the evidence, to discriminate between the genuine and the phoney. And they taught us how to write English prose. Exams were, in those days, almost entirely based on essays. Multiple-choice questions had yet to arrive from America. So we had to master the art of essay writing, and we had to get the hang of 'exam technique' – the ability to present such facts as we had learned in a way that would make them appear to be merely well-chosen examples from our vast range of knowledge.

Essay questions were sometimes astonishingly sophisticated. One in particular, part of an O-level history exam on the English Civil War, at first seemed so mind-bogglingly difficult that it has stuck in my mind to this day: 'Is Puritanism recurrent?' My first reaction when confronted with this was that I couldn't in a million years write an essay on such a theme. But on further reflection, I realised that it presented an ideal opportunity for applying 'exam technique' – and for indulging in generalised waffle.

It was our English teacher, Raymond O'Malley, whom I most admired and who taught me most, not just about literature but also about morality and about the connections between the two. He had written a much-praised book about his experiences as a crofter in the Scottish Highlands where, because he was a conscientious objector, he had been sent during the Second World War. Malley, as he was known at school, was a person of great sweetness and patience, with a passion for literature and a strong belief in the merits of simplicity. He would often try to make us rewrite a passage of prose in fewer words, without losing complexity or comprehensibility.

It was a joy to be taught by him.

Most pupils at Dartington left the school after taking O- or A-levels. In my year only three of us (all girls) stayed on to take university entrance exams (which in those days were independent of national exams). Theo was trying to get into Oxford to read history, while Hilary (with whom I had written satirical verses) and I were aiming to do English at Cambridge. There were very few places for women at Oxbridge at that time (I think the ratio of men to women was eleven to one) so the competition was fierce. Malley, who had managed to get several former students into Cambridge, was so convinced that we would both succeed that he discouraged us from even trying any other university – certainly not Oxford, about whose English department he was very disparaging.

As it turned out, I was the only one of us who failed to get in, or even to get an interview. I was bitterly disappointed (particularly as I had achieved the best A-level results of the three of us). Malley, too, seemed genuinely upset. On the day the results were announced, I lay on my bed for most of the afternoon, feeling miserable. Every half an hour or so, Malley would interrupt his lessons and come to my room to comfort me.

On the following day, I left the school for good. Malley accompanied me to Totnes railway station to see me off. As we parted – I remember it was pouring with rain – he said something which I've never forgotten but which, perhaps, he said to all his long-term pupils: 'We don't often get students like you.' About ten years later, I went to visit him in Cambridge where he was then living and though he was friendly enough, he barely remembered me. That, I realised, was the way it went with teachers and pupils: individual teachers are uniquely important in pupils' lives, while in a teacher's life, past pupils more often than not form a kind of blur.

I discovered something else about Malley that was faintly disillusioning. A great many of his insights into literature, and of the interpretations and appraisals of poems and novels which I had found so inspiring, turned out to derive, more or less verbatim, from the books of the renowned Cambridge lecturer and critic F.R. Leavis. Malley had been one of Leavis's most ardent disciples. Meanwhile, I had married a writer and critic, John Gross, who devoted many pages of his book *The Rise and Fall of the Man of Letters* to arguing – convincingly, in my view – that Leavis, for all his powers of discernment, was a damaging and constricting influence on students of literature, a tyrannical layer-down of literary laws. None of this, though, detracts from Malley's wonderful qualities as a teacher, or as a man.

I felt very sad during my final train journey back from Devon to London – partly because of my failure to get into Cambridge, and partly because of saying goodbye to Malley; mostly, though, because I was leaving behind a place that, for eight years, had become an alternative home. Though I had resented the school's hands-off educational philosophy and disliked the general laxity of the atmosphere, I had nevertheless been very lucky to be a pupil at Dartington. All its teachers and staff had been unfailingly kind and welcoming. They had acted as role models for fair-mindedness and unsnobbishness. I was only dimly aware, for example, that the English class system was still going strong and that racial prejudice still persisted, even in England.

Dartington had given me a sense of belonging – the feeling of being part of a group, or a circle, which, it seems to me, is one of the greatest sources of human happiness. By contrast, a friend of mine, a girl of the same age and from a similar background, who had been sent to a traditional girls' public school, had been made to feel socially inferior by one or two of the securely English, upper-class girls there. At that age, even slight condescension can have long-lasting effects. This could never have happened at Dartington, where we were at all times treated as equals.

III

Paris

There was one Oxbridge college which had not yet held its entrance exams for the following academic year – St Anne's College, Oxford. So after attending a 'crammer' in London for two or three weeks, I sat the exam. This time I was summoned for an interview and, to my delight, and that of my parents, I got a place.

Nevertheless, when the time came, I nearly didn't go. I had decided that, for my gap year (or what was left of it), it would be a good idea to go to Paris to improve my French. I duly signed up to the well-known course for foreigners, the Cours Civilisation Française, at the Sorbonne and was enrolled as a boarder at the Alliance Française, a reputable establishment where people from all over the world came to learn French as a second language. My mother accompanied me to Paris and left me there.

I don't remember much about the Alliance Française because, as it turned out, I spent very little time there. What I do recall is that the evening meal, served in a vast communal hall, was the high point of the day. Dozens of eager students buzzed around trying to communicate with one another. What they were eager about was not so much dining as dating. Naturally no one, including me, wanted to be alone in Paris.

I did in fact have two horrible dates with two young Frenchmen whom I met at the Sorbonne. One was a tall, skinny, academic type, with dark receding hair; the other was stocky with a fairish crew-cut and a loud laugh. What they had in common was a high-handed assumption that my agreeing to have a glass of wine with them gave them carte blanche to pounce on me, press themselves against me and maul me about. It was not so much sexual harassment as attempted rape. In those days it would not have occurred to anyone to report such encounters to any authorities, least of all to the police. But these incidents completely put me off having so much as a cup of coffee with any kind of Frenchman again – even in the interests of practising my French.

As it happened, I was soon otherwise engaged, in every sense of the word. A few weeks after arriving in Paris, I was having supper at one of the long trestle tables in the Alliance dining hall when a folded paper napkin was pushed in my direction. Inside was a wittily phrased – so I remember thinking – invitation to go out for a drink after the meal. I glanced around and saw an elegantly dressed, pleasant-looking student with a slightly too-low forehead, looking at me intently. At least he had the merit of not being French. 'Ok. A quick glass of wine at the nearest café,' I scribbled back, or words to that effect.

Reader, we fell in love over our first glass of wine, in a

crowded Parisian café – just like in the movies; or in the scores of romantic novels I had by that time absorbed. Soon we became engaged. And not long after that we moved in together. It was my first sexual relationship. My fiancé, who came from New York and was seven years older than me – he was already a graduate, from Cornell University – turned out to be quite rich. He rented a small flat in a charming street on the Left Bank and we both decamped from the Alliance Française. I didn't at that point tell my parents what I was up to, so I had to go back to the Alliance quite often to collect my mail.

So much for improving my French, though I did still continue to attend a few lectures at the Sorbonne. My fiancé, meanwhile, who was hoping to become an actor, spent much of his time doing something I had never before heard of – 'working out' in a gym. He was a fervent 'body builder', an ambition I regarded as some-what undignified and narcissistic. There were very few gyms in Paris at the time so he had to travel for miles to the nearest one. Another point of friction was the way he sometimes used the word 'Jew': to him it served as a derogatory adjective. An example of this, which has stuck in my mind, took place on the platform of a Metro station. 'Why', I heard him hiss under his breath, 'is this Jew train so late?'

However, this usage reflected the milieu from which he came, Upper East side New York, rather than anti-Semitism on his part – or are the two inseparable? When his haute couture mother came over to visit him, she asked, so he told me afterwards, whether I had had a 'nose job' – another phenomenon of which I had till then been ignorant.

Despite these discordant notes, we were determined to marry as soon as possible. A week or so before our spell in Paris was due to end, I wrote to my mother informing her that I no longer had any wish to go to Oxford. She immediately got on a train to Paris to try to talk me out of this – as she saw it – absurd decision. After much arguing and pleading, she persuaded me to strike a bargain: I would try Oxford for one term; if I still wanted to marry at the end of it, she would raise no further objections. Wise woman.

So my fiancé and I parted. There were still a few weeks before term began. I spent them with my parents in Frankfurt, occupied from morning till night either in writing long letters to, or reading long letters from, New York.

Oxford – St Anne's College

I had been very apprehensive about meeting the other girls at St Anne's College – they were bound, I thought, to be fiercely intellectual and frighteningly well informed. I envisaged all manner of highbrow conversations about politics and literature in which I would barely be able to hold my own, over meals or in the junior common room. There were only five women's colleges at Oxford, so their intake, I assumed, must represent the country's crème de la crème. To my relief, but also disappointment, the reality was very different.

St Anne's at that time did not yet have a central residential hall, so students were farmed out to various lodging houses or hostels near the main college building in north Oxford. There were eight girls in the house to which I had been allocated and none of them were in the least intimidating. Indeed, they all seemed startlingly unprepossessing. As far as I could tell, they had no interest whatever in current affairs or politics, and I never saw any of them read a newspaper. They didn't even seem particularly enthused by literature – not, anyway, by the kinds of novels – Thomas Hardy, George Eliot, D.H. Lawrence, Dostoevsky – that I had been reading at school and since. It's true that most of these particular girls happened to be studying modern languages, and even those studying English were more focused on linguistics. The Oxford English syllabus was, at that time, based largely on the study of Old and Middle English.

But the insular and inward-looking attitude of my co-lodgers was baffling. What they liked doing best was sitting around in their bedrooms drinking cups of tea. They barely left the confines of the college. One girl, whose room was adjacent to mine, and who became a life-long friend, did allow herself to be dragged off to listen to a debate at the Oxford Union; but that was exceptional. I see now that attending a co-educational, progressive school had helped me to become more worldly and perhaps broad-minded; the other girls would no doubt catch up with me or indeed overtake me in later years. But at the time their intellectual narrowness was a surprise.

But then I must have seemed equally surprising

to them. When I arrived at St Anne's, I was wearing a diamond engagement ring; every morning at the breakfast table I would receive two long letters by airmail; on Mondays the number would sometimes rise to five. I wore relatively trendy clothes and didn't require constant cups of tea. Certainly I was regarded, for the first few months at least, as an exotic interloper. I had to turn myself into a kind of joke-figure in order to deflect their disapproval.

But life in our hostel, though not intellectually stimulating, soon became psychologically compelling. One of the girls, it emerged, was a nasty troublemaker – a kind of Mrs Danvers in our midst. Perhaps the ratio of eight to one reflects the average distribution of more or less 'good' people to more or less 'bad' people. This bad girl's appearance was, as often in such cases, wholly deceptive: she had a pleasant, round, open face and thick blonde hair tied into a bun; and she had a somewhat stocky, matronly figure. On first acquaintance she seemed exceptionally trustworthy – someone to confide in. She had been headgirl at a large grammar school.

But it soon became clear that what she was after was power – she wanted to have us all under her thumb. To this end she used the age-old tactic of 'divide and rule', telling each of us things that the others had said about us, always with her own subversive spin, thus breeding suspicion and ill-feeling all round. Like most such people, she professed to the highest moral principles and she disapproved of a whole array of activities – particularly of people enjoying themselves.

Again, like other such characters (I have subsequently come across one or two similar people in my own life, and many more in books), she had a very strong personality. Everyone was always anxiously trying to please and appease her. The atmosphere in our hostel came to resemble a cross between that of a tea party and a police state. It took about a year for us to get wise to the tactics of our live-in totalitarian. The process led to endless fascinating discussions and dissections of her character.

In our third year, this same girl suddenly and miraculously acquired a boyfriend. Needless to say, she immediately started behaving in exactly the way that she most disapproved of in others. She literally let her hair down; she and the boy would disappear into her room, locking the door behind them (disgraceful) and stay there all afternoon (unheard of). I suppose this should be regarded as a happy ending.

The syllabus of the English Honours School was another surprise. Nobody had told me (though of course I should have found out for myself) that it would be quite so heavily biased in favour of linguistics. St Anne's was particularly strong in this field. It wasn't enough to study Old and Middle English texts with the aid of a crib; we had to struggle with the declensions and conjugations of these two languages which are as different from one another as they both are from modern English. I felt as though I had been unwittingly bounced into a crash course in Dutch and Danish (which would have been much more useful). The study of philology is undoubtedly a fascinating field, but unfortunately I found it very tedious; it actually blinded me to the quality of that great Anglo-Saxon epic Beowulf, and marred my enjoyment of the marvellous Middle English poetry we were studying.

This emphasis on linguistics had its origins in the fierce debate, which raged at the university at the end of the nineteenth and beginning of the twentieth century, about the suitability of English as an academic subject. Wasn't literature, many dons argued, a leisure activity rather than an academic discipline – 'mere chatter about Shelley', as someone at the time put it? There is, of course, some force in this argument, and it was to imbue the subject with more scholarly rigour and backbone that so much language study was introduced into the course. For the same reason, the literary works included on the syllabus did not go beyond 1832. (One could take an optional paper on more recent literature, but I was too lazy to sign up for an unnecessary exam.)

St Anne's had excellent English tutors – in particular some eminent philologists (all women, of course) – whose interests were certainly not confined to premodern literature. Indeed, it was thanks to one of the younger tutors that I had the most thrilling, albeit extracurricular, literary experience of my time at Oxford. She introduced me to a novel that had recently come out in Paris and that was, at the time, officially banned both in France and in England – Nabokov's *Lolita*. Somehow, she had managed to get hold of an 'underground' copy, published by the avant-garde Olympia Press. I thought it the most brilliant and moving novel I had ever read.

Tutorials with a man

All our tutorials were held at St Anne's, except during one term, when we were farmed out to a male tutor, at a man's college. This caused great excitement and anticipation. There were normally two students at each tutorial. My tutorial partner, Joan Newman, was a clever, jovial girl who later became the rector of an Episcopalian church in the US. The don to whom we were assigned was called Ian Jack, a lecturer at Brasenose College.

The first thing this man did when we – two nervous, overawed nineteen-year-olds – had settled into the leather armchairs of his spacious study was to pick up a book from his desk and wave it in the air. 'Have you read Spencer's novel?' he asked us. There was a momentary stunned silence during which I wondered whether Edmund Spenser's *The Faerie Queene* could conceivably be described as a novel. Luckily, Joan, a more extrovert person than me, answered first. 'I didn't know Spenser had written a novel,' she said boldly. 'Of course he didn't – I just wanted to see what you would say,' replied the tutor. 'This book', he proclaimed, still waving it above his head, 'is a highly commended study of Augustan satire. It's written by me.'

The other things I remember about our first tutorial is that Mr Jack spent a great deal of it chatting on the phone; also that his small children would from time to time burst into the room and out again. For our next tutorial he set us an essay on Wordsworth. I was determined, as was Joan, to show this obnoxious don that we were not to be trifled with. So I worked extremely hard in the library all week, writing a very long and, as I thought, penetrating study of Romantic poetry.

It was the usual practice in tutorials that one of the two students read her essay aloud; it would then be discussed for the rest of the session. The other student, meanwhile, would hand hers in to be read by the tutor and returned the following week. At our tutorial on Wordsworth, it fell to Joan to read her essay, while I left mine lying on Mr Jack's desk.

When our next tutorial came round a week later, I was eagerly anticipating his reaction to my magnum opus – hoping, of course, for praise. But it was lying in the exact spot where I had left it. He hadn't, as he told me, had time to read it. Nor had he read it in time for any of our subsequent tutorials. My thoughts about Wordsworth remained on his desk, week after week, gathering dust. At the end of term, I have no doubt, he chucked the essay into his waste-paper basket. Needless to say, this experience didn't do much to encourage hard work. From then on, I did just enough to get by.

No don today could get away with this kind of high-handed, not to say bone-idle, way of doing his or her job. But in the 1950s and early 60s, Ian Jack's behaviour was not untypical of the dismissive attitude of male academics towards women students. (He subsequently, to my astonishment, obtained a chair at Cambridge.)

Philosophy and politics

Luckily, non-literary activities and lectures proved more rewarding. Most memorably, I attended the wonderful inaugural lecture – 'Two Concepts of Liberty' – by Isaiah Berlin (he had been made Chichele Professor of Social and Political Theory). I probably didn't understand it all, but in so far as I did, the lecture impressed me as being profoundly right about everything.

By a stroke of good fortune, I was soon to become personally acquainted with Isaiah Berlin and, like everyone else who met him, I was transfixed by his dazzling erudition and his exuberant conversation, as well as by his evident kindness. His idiosyncratic way of talking – with its stream of adjectives: 'aloof, Olympian, chilly, detached', and its crescendos of phrases that usually came in threes: 'Where do we come from? How did we get here? Where are we going?' – sprang, I presume, from his eagerness to cover all aspects and nuances of a subject.

Many years later, in 1979, he reluctantly agreed to do an interview with me for the *Observer* newspaper, on which I was then employed. Isaiah hated talking about himself, he told me, but he was willing to talk about a subject which was preoccupying him at the time: 'Alienation'. Help! I had never even heard of Alienation. Luckily, the date of the interview was about two months away, at the end of the summer. So I had plenty of time to mug it up. Google, unfortunately, had not yet been invented so I spent more or less every waking minute of the summer – at the breakfast table, on beaches, in restaurants, not to mention pillow talk – boring people with questions about this elusive topic; I read all I could find about the Russian critic Vissarion Belinsky, who seemed to be Alienation's main proponent.

When the day of the interview arrived, I took with me a list of what I hoped were pertinent questions. But I had hardly opened my mouth before Isaiah exclaimed: 'Alienation – no, no, no. Let's not talk about that!' He had obviously forgotten all about his condition for our interview. Disaster! I was reduced to asking questions such as 'What are your favourite books?'

Being the great man he was, Isaiah overlooked the banality of my questions and spoke brilliantly and unstoppably for about an hour about the purpose and impact of literature, ranging widely in all directions. 'Great novels', he for example said, 'convey the true moral centre of gravity of human predicaments; they can expand the frontiers of experience and open windows as events in one's life may not have done.'

I wove his words (which I had of course recorded – they were often fiendishly difficult to disentangle) into a long soliloquy, leaving out my own idiotic interjections. This peculiar interview was duly published in the *Observer*. No newspaper today would dream of publishing such a highbrow monologue.

A few weeks after arriving at Oxford, I made friends with a very good-looking undergraduate. We sat next to each other at a lecture, and after swapping impressions about the technique of the lecturer, he asked me to tea. An invitation to tea, in those days, was the equivalent of a first date. The boy was called Julian Ayer and he was the son of the eminent philosopher A.J. (Freddie) Ayer. We began to see each other more and more often and I began to think less and less about my fiancé in America.

Isaiah Berlin

It hadn't taken long for me to behave just as faithlessly – though on a very mundane level – as Criseyde (Cressida) in Chaucer's wonderful narrative poem *Troilus and Criseyde* which we were then studying in its original Middle English. Criseyde, when parted from her Trojan suitor Troilus, to whom she had sworn eternal love, takes no time at all to transfer her affections to a new admirer, the Greek warrior Diomedes.

I sent my engagement ring back to America, accompanied by an apologetic, self-justifying letter. My fiancé wrote back saying that he found it incredible that anyone could be so shallow. He had thrown the ring, he said, into the Hudson River. (I've always wondered whether he really did this.) Our engagement ended exactly as my mother had anticipated – and hoped.

It was through Julian that I met Isaiah Berlin and various other Oxford intellectual grandees, in particular his parents. As it happened, three people could be described as Julian's parents, though he did not know this at the time, and nor did I. His official parents, Freddie and Renee Ayer, were now divorced. Julian still saw a lot of Freddie, the man he assumed was his father and who had indeed been a very good father. However, there were rumours that his real father was another distinguished philosopher, Stuart Hampshire, whom Renee married in 1961. I always vehemently denied these rumours. Despite my unconventional education, I had never heard of children being born out of wedlock, or rather into wedlock – the very idea seemed preposterous. When people pointed out that Julian looked very like Stuart Hampshire, I insisted that he looked just like his mother (which he did). Julian himself had no doubt that Ayer was his father.

Years later, Renee, who became a much better friend after Julian and I parted than she had been during the course of our relationship, told me that when they finally informed Julian that Stuart was his real father, he, Julian, had flown into a hysterical rage (as well he might) and had broken all their valuable Victorian glass.

My involvement with Julian lasted for a year. Very soon after we started going out together, Renee, a very manipulative and controlling character (she had reputedly locked A.J. Ayer into his study for days at a time to ensure that he would finish writing his first, highly acclaimed book *Language, Truth and Logic*), insisted on taking me to London to see the birth-control pioneer, Dr Helena Wright. The aim was to fit me up with a contraceptive device. This gynaecological trip took place before Julian and I had even embarked on a sexual relationship.

It was a memorably horrible experience. Helena Wright, a stout, hearty, feminist battleaxe of a doctor, examined me in a very painful way. At the time I thought this was normal, though later I realised that gynaecological examinations could be carried out without causing any pain at all. Next she informed me that I had 'the womb of a nine-year-old child', an assessment that preyed on my mind for many years to come (it turned out to be nonsense); finally she inquired whether I knew what an orgasm was, and when I said yes, she asked me to describe it – was it like a sneeze, did I think?

Why Julian's mother had arranged this appointment (though I'm sure she didn't anticipate that it would be so unpleasant for me), I didn't at the time understand. Later, I realised that it was a very typical act of aggression masquerading as sensible, helpful concern. This premature contraception, so to speak, was, I think, calculated to throw Julian and me off balance. Renee, though she never said so, did not approve of me as a long-term prospect for her beloved only son. She was hoping that Julian would find someone much better connected than a Jewish girl from nowhere. She would quite often say things to Julian that were designed to put him off me. One such thing, I recall, involved eye make-up. The fact that I used black eyeliner under my eye, claimed Renee, proved that I was not quite *comme il faut*. This was particularly unfair as black eye-liner all around the eyes was very much in vogue at the time.

In subsequent years, whenever I met Isaiah Berlin socially, we would invariably get round to discussing the strange personality of Julian's mother. Both A.J. Ayer and Stuart Hampshire had been close friends of Isaiah's, and he had spent many years studying Renee Ayer-Hampshire's contradictory character. We would, for example, exchange anecdotes about her overpowering generosity: she would shower people with so many gifts, even when they were guests in her house, that they ended up feeling guilty and oppressed. Or she would heap so much praise on someone that he or she couldn't help suspecting that she was enjoying some kind of private joke. Renee was the daughter of Colonel Thomas Orde-Lees, an intrepid member of Ernest Shackleton's team on his failed Antarctic trip of 1914. She herself had, in her twenties, single-handedly crossed Japan on a motorbike.

On the whole, though, all three of Julian's parents were extremely kind to me and I was often invited, with Julian, to lunches and dinners attended by various members of Oxford's intellectual elite. I hardly ever said a word on these occasions, being overawed by the brilliant small talk and the sophisticated repartee on all sides. I couldn't help noticing, though, how much of this conversation consisted of gossip and character analysis – or, more accurately, character assassination. Friends and foes alike were subjected to merciless dissection, often with the aid of Sigmund Freud. The guests themselves were by no means spared. No sooner had one of them left the room than those remaining would tear into him or her, enumerating his or her flaws and transgressions.

Having been brought up, both by my parents and by my school, to believe that talking about people behind their backs was ill-mannered, I was disconcerted by such torrents of indiscretion. I remember being particularly taken aback at a lunch party to which an undergraduate, regarded as the most gifted student of our year, had been invited. This boy had to leave early, so he politely excused himself and departed before the coffee was served. As soon as he was out of earshot, one of the other guests, a distinguished professor, announced loudly to the rest of the company that he (the brilliant undergraduate) was not nearly as 'good' (which in Oxford-speak meant clever) as he was reputed to be: on the contrary, he had a superficial, journalistic mind. I was shocked then, and am still shocked now, that this assessment was made in the presence of Julian and me about one of our contemporaries. It was bound to prejudice us, and it did.

Why did these eminent academics, who were not normally unkind or insensitive, behave in such a scurrilous way? Perhaps, having lived their lives in an atmosphere of intense intellectual competitiveness, they had developed this highhanded and hard-hearted way of showing off to each other – of trumping each other with sharp insights and intimate revelations. In the process they seemed to have lost sight of how ungentlemanly they sounded to people outside their ivory-tower cocoon. But this was half a century ago – the world has now gone almost too far in the opposite direction, constantly worrying about everyone's sensitivities. I wonder, though, whether Oxford dons still carry on in this unfeeling way when they're talking among themselves.

Soon after arriving at Oxford, I had joined the university's Labour Club. It never entered my head to associate with a political party that was not left of centre. I had swallowed whole the notion that the Left represented all the virtues – decency, tolerance, fairness, compassion – and that the Right was selfish, inconsiderate and snobbish.

That was certainly the assumption of most of the adults at Dartington Hall when I was a pupil there, and it has been the view of *bien pensant* opinion ever since. The fact that regimes of the far Left all over the world have been no less murderous (though perhaps less sadistic) than those of the far Right, and that fascists first learned the techniques of dictatorship from communists, does not seem to have dented this belief.

I clung to the view that the Left commanded the moral high ground for many years, despite the evidence of my own eyes and ears. A student trip to the annual Labour Party conference did not shake my faith, although it was an eye-opening experience. Sitting in the gallery surrounded by screaming activists, I could not hear a word of what the speakers below were saying. The veins in the necks of these rank-and-file leftists bulged with class hatred. Any opinions that were halfway moderate were anathema to them. At the same time, the party grandees who were invited to address the Labour Club proved uninspiring. I remember looking forward to speeches by Denis Healey and James Callaghan and being astonished that they talked entirely in clichés.

Even when, in the 1960s, the Labour education secretary Anthony Crosland introduced the policy, so damaging to the chances of clever working-class children, of eliminating selection and converting all state schools into comprehensives ('If it's the last thing I do, I'm going to destroy every last fucking grammar school in England'), I still stuck with Labour; and in the 1979 election, when I was convinced, along with the majority of the country, that a change of government was urgently needed to rescue Britain from economic disaster, I baulked at putting my cross against the Tory candidate, opting for the Liberal instead. My husband John, when I confessed this last-minute loss of nerve as we were leaving the polling station, merely remarked: 'Middle-class guilt runs very deep.'

It was only in the 1980s, while I was working at the *Observer*, that I realised quite how much damage had been done by liberal/left politics in this period. I vividly remember a conversation with my friend Anthony Howard, who was then deputy editor of the paper (and who should have become its editor), during which I admitted my admiration for Mrs Thatcher. He staggered backwards in dismay, as though I had made a rude noise.

Rhodes scholars
My time at Oxford would probably have been

intellectually more rewarding if I had not been continuously preoccupied – just as I had been in previous years and would be in subsequent years – with 'love interest'. After my involvement with Julian (who was tragically killed in the tsunami which hit Thailand in 2004), I had several further infatuations, mainly with American Rhodes scholars. These scholars – around 30 of them are selected each year – are chosen not just for their academic attainments but also for their all-round abilities. Since they have already graduated from their home universities, they are older and liable to be more mature than English undergraduates. The last of my Rhodes scholar involvements is a rather curious story.

I can't remember how I first met Kris (he was of Swedish descent): most probably at a lecture, as he was also studying English. He had a round baby-face, a crew-cut and small, blue, deep-set eyes. He looked like everyone's idea of a fresh-faced US marine straight out of naval college. He was also the shyest person I have ever met, before or since. I am attracted to shy people and we somehow got talking, though he didn't say much. He lived in California, he told me, and enjoyed boxing (I later learned that he was a boxing blue, in other words, on the Oxford boxing team) and playing the guitar. He blushed a great deal. I often wondered how on earth he had managed to win a scholarship – not that he was unintelligent but it was difficult to imagine him answering questions in an interview without getting tongue-tied.

We became friends and he soon started visiting me in my room several times a week. He mentioned that he had a girlfriend back home to whom he was intending to return. Nevertheless, we spent a great deal of time kissing. Indeed, except for intermittent conversations about Chaucer or Dryden, that is what we mainly did. These kissing afternoons went on for many weeks. Then one day we decided to drive to London and spend the night together. We couldn't do this in the digs in which I was then living. I can't remember what prompted such a bold deviation from our usual routine, but off we drove, speaking very little on the way, and booked into a dingy hotel in the suburbs of London.

It was already late, so we immediately got into bed. After that things happened – or rather didn't happen – very quickly. In fact, nothing happened. Before you could say Jack Robinson, Kris was lying with his back to me, apparently asleep. He hadn't even kissed me goodnight. Next morning we drove back to Oxford in silence. Whether Kris had been overcome by nerves, or whether he couldn't, at the last moment, bring himself to be unfaithful to his girlfriend, or whether he had suddenly gone off me, or whether he had experienced a very discreet premature ejaculation, remains a mystery.

We never again talked about this incident. We resumed our former kissing sessions shortly afterwards and continued until the end of term, and the end of both our spells at Oxford. His last words when we said goodbye at Oxford railway station, were 'I have learned so much from you.' I don't know whether he meant about literature or about life, or whether he was just being nice.

Fifteen or so years later I was sitting in a friend's house

when I saw a 78-inch record lying nearby. The name Kris Kristofferson was printed in large letters on its cover. 'That's funny,' I said, 'I once knew someone called Kris Kristofferson.' It couldn't be the same man. I idly turned the record over. There was my Kris, his unmistakeable little eyes looking out from a round bearded face. He had become one of the world's leading country and western singers. Later he was to become a famous film star as well. (Since my brief friendship with him took place more than half a century ago, I feel that 'kiss and tell' constraints no longer apply.)

Infatuations apart, though, my time as an undergraduate had by and large been disappointing. I had somehow managed not to grasp the opportunities either for carefree enjoyment or for academic learning. Most of my time seems to have been spent sitting aimlessly in cafés and in college rooms, smoking and drinking cups of coffee, rather than in libraries, concentrating. It felt as though I had floated through this period without quite existing. (The feeling that I don't really exist is something I often experience – perhaps most people do.)

After taking my final exams (to my great relief, I obtained a second-class degree – there were no division into 2.1s and 2.2s at Oxford in those days), I had no clear career plan. Very few women at that time did. I knew there was such a thing as the Oxford University Appointments Board, but I had assumed it was intended primarily for men. Since my parents firmly believed that I ought to have a proper qualification, I agreed to stay in Oxford for another year and get a Diploma of Education.

I got the diploma, but it was a useless course: it taught me neither how to relate to pupils nor how to teach my subject. The only worthwhile thing about it was the term spent as a student teacher in a London comprehensive school. But I was too nervous and inexperienced to be an effective teacher. I recall how embarrassed I felt when the book from which I was reading aloud to the class trembled in my hands for all to see. And anyway, I wanted to do something more glamorous.

IV

Jobs

When I returned to London, however, I found that, in my case at least, an Honours degree did nothing to help in finding a job. Of course, having gone to Oxford brought enormous indirect advantages, particularly for someone like me who was not English-born. In the first place, it supplied me with some much-needed social cachet, which greatly increased my confidence. And it taught me how to converse with intellectuals, which was to prove very useful in my later work as a literary journalist. It also revealed to me the subtle gradations of the English class system (though I suppose I could have acquired the same knowledge by reading Evelyn Waugh). Most importantly, though, attending an ancient university gave me, through its buildings, its institutions and its atmosphere, a very satisfying sense of continuity and connectedness with the history of the country that was now my home.

Like many English graduates, particularly women, I thought that a career in publishing was probably what I was best fitted for. I sent off piles of letters of application, but the only job I was offered was as a filing clerk at the publishing company, Hutchinson. So I took it. The people I was working for had reached senior positions, not by spending three years at a university, but by using that time to climb up the career ladder. My immediate boss, Mrs Stockwell, was a strident, thick-skinned, middle-aged woman who, I was soon to learn, was disliked and feared in the office. And my very first assignment was to mend her bra. Its strap had snapped on the way to work. Could I, she barked, sew it back on, but first run out and buy needle and thread. Luckily I had picked up the rudiments of sewing from one of my parents' housekeepers, so I was able to perform this task. Her bra, I remember, was beige.

My other tasks were hardly more appealing: looking through old publishing contracts and moving them from one file to another, sorting out bits of paper on Mrs Stockwell's desk and making cups of tea for her. Meanwhile, my private life was equally dreary. I was living in a bedsit in West Hampstead and spending a great deal of time eating biscuits. Since I didn't know many people in London – my closest friends seemed all to have moved to America and my parents were living in Frankfurt – I would often go to the cinema on my own.

My second job was better. Despite not having learned shorthand or typing, I was taken on as secretary to the advertising manager of *Encounter*, the highly regarded cultural and political (right-of-centre) monthly magazine. My duties consisted of taking dictation (fast longhand) of letters about advertising space and typing them up, tidying the office and making cups of tea.

After a few months of this I had a lucky break. Someone was needed, at short notice, to translate an article from German. I was known to speak German, so I was summoned from the advertising department and asked to do it. This raised my profile in the editorial department and drew me to the notice of John Gross, at that time a Cambridge don and a part-time editor of *Encounter*. When, some months later, the literary editor of the *Observer* was looking for a secretary, John – who reviewed books for the paper and whom at that stage I hardly knew – recommended me, and I was given the job.

In my twenties

The *Observer*

The *Observer* was at the time probably the most respected newspaper in England. It was a 'must-read' for anyone interested in culture and politics, particularly foreign politics, and it had strong and controversial, left-leaning but not party-political, views that reflected the beliefs of its editor David Astor. Astor, who was born into the immensely wealthy Anglo-American Astor dynasty, had struck out on his own into journalism. As owner/editor he had recruited a line-up of authoritative commentators and talented writers, including George Orwell. One of them, Malcolm Muggeridge, an early television guru, described the *Observer* as 'a home for intellectual drunks'; and indeed a great deal of the senior staff's time was spent in nearby pubs. But this didn't seem to affect the quality of the paper.

Its book pages, in particular, were admired for their consistently high standards – it was regarded as an honour to be asked to review for them. For me, the *Observer* represented an exciting new world. And it gave me a start for what eventually became a career in literary and arts journalism. I stayed at the paper for almost twenty years, the last four as woman's editor in charge of a section intended to appeal to women. It was a post which later, with the advance of feminism, became extinct.

My new boss was Terence Kilmartin, and it would be hard to imagine a more charming, more cultured or more civilised man with whom to share an office. He was also extremely handsome. As Clive James – who became a regular contributor to the paper soon after I joined – put it: 'Kilmartin was as good-looking as a man can be without ceasing to look intelligent as well.' He had already been the paper's literary editor for twelve years and he was to stay in the job for another 22 – a total of 34 years. Throughout that period he was regarded as the best literary editor in town.

Terry (as he was known) was an autodidact. He had been brought up in Ireland, one of eight children, by a widowed mother of modest means – too modest to send him to university. After attending a good Catholic school, he had gone to France as English tutor to a French family. In the process he developed a lifelong interest in things French, particularly its literature. He became an award-winning translator of several important French works. For the last twenty years or so of his life he worked obsessively on a revised translation of Marcel Proust's *In Search of Lost Time*.

Terry had met David Astor while they were both serving on a secret wartime mission in occupied France in 1944. According to rumour, Terry had saved Astor's life; according to Terry, all he had done was drag Astor, who had been wounded, from under one tree, where he had been sheltering, to another tree a few yards away, where he would be safer from enemy detection. Terry probably risked his own life doing this – but he would never have said so. He was at all times self-effacing and reticent. After the war, Astor offered him a job as a reporter on the *Observer*.

I was to work for Terry for fifteen years – as secretary, then as assistant and, for about seven years, as deputy. Since there were never more than three people working in our office, my promotion to deputy was purely nominal

– perhaps in recognition of the fact that Terry's preoccupation with Proust meant that he often left me to get on with the books pages on my own.

Right from my first day, Terry gallantly treated me more as a colleague than as a secretary. He would ask for my views on books and reviews and even sometimes invite me to accompany him to the pub, along with literary friends and reviewers who would often visit our office to inspect the new books on the shelves. But this was unusual. More often than not, secretaries, even in the world of journalism, were treated as though they didn't have opinions or feelings.

Whenever anything of moment occurred – a resignation or a falling-out or a scandal – either in the world at large or in the intriguing realm of office politics, the men on the paper's staff (there were very few women in executive positions at that time) would huddle in small conspiratorial groups to discuss the ins and outs of the event; they would make quite sure they were out of earshot of any secretary sitting nearby. The assumption was that we, like children, were not sufficiently discreet or balanced to hear the lowdown of what was going on – *pas devant les enfants*. Even Terry behaved in this infuriating way. I would be reduced to asking him to let me in on what the 'grown-ups' had been saying. But I only dared to do this after a year or so into the job, when we had become friends.

Two examples of the offensive way in which males – who in other respects may have been charming – behaved towards secretaries stick in my mind. In both cases, as it

Terence Kilmartin, literary
editor of the *Observer* for 34 years

happens, the men were well-known. One was the *Observer*'s chief reviewer, Philip Toynbee. I had only been in my new job for about a week when Toynbee – perhaps he had just surfaced from a pub lunch – made one of his rare visits to the office. Suddenly he walked over to where I was sitting and prodded my breasts several times with a pencil. He did this quite openly, with a pleased grin – as though he had done something clever – in front of various people who were standing around.

He also, I remember, dropped some ash from his cigarette onto my jumper. Those were days when nearly everyone smoked – indeed, to be a non-smoker was regarded as rather old-maidish; to talk with a cigarette drooping from the corner of your mouth was a sign of sophistication. Overflowing ashtrays adorned every desk on the editorial floor.

The other incident involved Anthony Crosland, then minister of education. Terry and I were both leaving the *Observer* building when Crosland, a good friend of Terry's, happened to be entering it. They greeted each other warmly and Terry introduced me. Crosland didn't respond but he looked me up and down and, addressing himself to Terry, asked him: 'Is this your new au pair girl?' Other secretaries on the paper suffered from similarly insulting behaviour.

Very soon after arriving at the *Observer*, the paper's prominent theatre critic, Kenneth Tynan, started asking me out. (He was recently divorced from the novelist Elaine Dundy and was soon to marry the beautiful Kathleen.) This was very flattering and we went on a number of dates, most memorably to a grand Lord Mayor's banquet – my first experience of a 'top people's' gathering – at which Tynan behaved rather childishly, throwing bread rolls and whispering loudly during the speeches. Very likely he only accepted the invitation in order to misbehave – *épater le bourgeois*. He also invited me to dinner at the exotic Café Royal, with its deep, red velvet seats and its louche atmosphere; I felt uncomfortably out of place in this former haunt of Oscar Wilde's.

Tynan was the kind of person who was permanently in the grip of an infatuation – as was I. But though I liked him very much, I did not in the slightest reciprocate his romantic interest. On one occasion he took me to his sumptuous flat in Mayfair, sat me down and put on a Barbra Streisand recording. 'If you don't weep when you hear this s-song,' he always spoke with a slight stammer, 'it will prove that you don't have a soul.' I remained dry-eyed.

Tynan was an odd combination of flamboyance and naivety. If he had possessed the opposite qualities – reticence and realism – he would have appealed to me more. But he was very sweet-natured and gentle, indeed gentlemanly, at any rate in my experience. On our last date, Ken begged me to come to his bedroom and just lie on the bed with him for a few minutes, nothing more, he promised. I reluctantly agreed, but when I saw that there was a large mirror on the ceiling above his four-poster bed I hastily retreated. (I was completely unaware of Ken's sado-masochistic leanings, about which I learned later.) Ken soon gave up on me, but we remained friends. I visited him in California just before his death from emphysema in 1980, at the age of 53. He was playing with his small son, an exquisitely beautiful child.

My duties as Terry's secretary, apart from answering the phone and making cups of tea, included opening parcels. Books of all shapes and sizes were sent to our office every day by publishers in the (usually vain) hope that they would be selected for review. The *Observer* carried, at best, two broadsheet book pages a week, so that out of approximately 50 new books, only a small percentage could be reviewed. (Many years later, when I was literary editor of the *Sunday Telegraph*, we would be allotted many more pages, giving the lie to the myth that book coverage went into steady decline.) Another of my duties was trotting back and forth to 'the stone', as the floor below, where the printers worked, was known. I would hand over typescripts – or handwritten manuscripts – to the typesetters; once the reviews were in type, the pages would be put together on stone slabs by the compositors.

These printers were immensely skilled and witty, many of them Cockneys. I was often sent down to beg the compositors to please try to squeeze just one more word – or even one more comma – into a review that was too long to fit in. At this point a compositor would invariably respond with one of many inventive variations on the phrase 'as the actress said to the bishop'. Indeed, the most frequently used word on the printers' floor was probably 'squeeze'. Most of the printers were very friendly, others were surly class warriors; in either case, it often struck me that, had they been brought up in middle-class homes, they might well have become doctors, lawyers or professors. When their craft became obsolete in the 1980s, many of them turned to taxi driving.

Proof-reading was, in those pre-computer days, an essential part of journalism (spell-check was undreamt of). The potential for errors and 'typos' to creep into an article at various stages of the process between its submission and its publication was huge. For a start, several of our reviewers wrote their pieces in well-nigh illegible handwriting. Others sent in typescripts disfigured by corrections, insertions and deletions which could easily be misread. Only a few took the trouble – and in the age of the typewriter there was a great deal of trouble involved – of handing in 'clean copy'. Anthony Burgess,

I remember, was one (he told me that he would retype his reviews again and again – whenever he made the slightest error – wasting masses of paper) and so were Kingsley Amis and Martin Amis. It was particularly distressing when typesetting errors were introduced into these perfectionists' immaculately presented reviews.

Since most book reviewers were not on the staff, it was my responsibility to send them proofs of their reviews (luckily the post in those days was reliable) so that they could phone in corrections. Occasionally it fell to me to deal with these corrections and also to help with proof-reading. But such tasks were strictly the responsibility of the assistant literary editor, at that time Irving Wardle, who was soon to become theatre critic of *The Times*. When he left, about a year after I arrived, I took over his job and a new secretary was appointed.

One of the incidental benefits of working on book review pages is that it is a way of continuing one's education. I learned more in the course of doing my job than I ever had at school or university (which admittedly is not saying much). Many of the country's most distinguished historians, philosophers, literary critics, scientists and novelists contributed to Terry's pages, and their reviews often contained more expertise and insight than the books they were assessing. It was a privilege to edit their articles and to talk to them about editorial details.

One of these contributors was John Gross, whom I had met briefly a year or so earlier. I came to admire him hugely – he was extraordinarily perceptive and knowledgeable about politics and culture in general, as well as about his own subject, literature – and then to fall in love with him. We were married in 1965. My parents liked John well enough, but my mother, I suspect, would have preferred me to marry a member of the landed gentry rather than a Jewish intellectual.

John Gross

Our first home was a rented one-bedroom furnished basement flat in St John's Wood. It had, I remember, hospital-green walls and a gas fire heater with a meter attached, into which you had to feed coins. All the furnishings – carpets, curtains, cushions, bedspreads – were in varying shades of green. Despite these surroundings, I took to married life immediately. Being part of an official couple seemed to me the ideal state of being. I relished both staying at home together and going out together. It never occurred either to John or to me to challenge our traditional roles: he performed such tasks as paying bills, arranging insurance and taking the rubbish out (though being a quintessential intellectual he was not much of a handyman); while I was quite happy – in those early months and in such a small flat – to do the cleaning and ironing.

I tried, more or less from scratch, to teach myself to cook by doggedly following recipes in magazines. We even gave a few very small dinner parties for friends. One of the first of these was a culinary disaster. John had invited a New York acquaintance who was spending a few days in London: the famously savage and much-feared theatre and film critic John Simon (born in 1925 and still going strong). Many highly regarded playwrights, among them Arthur Miller, Harold Pinter and David Mamet, are not highly regarded by him. But he is mainly known for his merciless assaults on actors' physical appearance. Of Elizabeth Taylor, for example, he wrote: 'Her entire performance, in contradistinction to her appearance, lacks weight'; of Barbra Streisand: 'Her nose cleaves the giant screen from East to West, bisects it from North to South.' Not surprisingly, he has been described as 'the world's nastiest critic'.

I had not met John Simon, but I assumed that someone so vitriolic must himself be physically disadvantaged, not to mention psychologically bitter and twisted. Not a bit of it. He had film-star good looks – tall, dark and hand-some – and was extremely genial, though in a dogmatic kind of way. I had bought avocado pears, a rare treat in those days – I had never bought one before. I cut them in half, and, having added a much-laboured-over vinaigrette, placed what seemed to me a perfect first course on our guest's plate. His avocado turned out to be as hard as a cricket ball – inedible. John Simon looked at me disdainfully: 'My dear, it's clear that you have no idea what you're doing.' It took me weeks to recover from this remark.

Just before I had my first child, we moved into a comfortable family house with a garden in West Hampstead. It cost, I remember, £11,000 (now it would be worth a hundred times more). We would not have been able to afford this house without the help of my parents. Though not especially wealthy, they were always willing to give me financial assistance when I needed it. I was, after all, their only child. The combination of parental help and a two-income household has meant that, throughout my life, I have been free from serious worries about money. The difference that such freedom makes to the quality of one's life is incalculable.

Editorial experience
Impressive though many of the *Observer*'s contributors were, I soon made the disillusioning discovery that quite a number of esteemed academics, as well as some professional writers and journalists, didn't write very well. Sorting out grammatical blunders, non-sequiturs and sloppy arguments was all part of the day's work, and I often wondered how people who produced such slipshod prose

had become eminent professors or renowned novelists. (Of course, writing fiction is very different from writing reviews – but there is surely some overlap.) Two notable examples stick in my mind. One was Angus Wilson, a highly successful novelist of the period. Wilson's reviews were dashed off in barely legible handwriting on scraps of paper torn from an exercise book. They contained no punctuation and very little by way of syntax or style – the same adjectives and phrases would appear on every page.

Transforming these scribbles into readable sentences required three stages: first to decipher the handwriting, then to crack the meaning and lastly to rewrite the whole thing in words and cadences that Angus Wilson himself might have used. Terry was brilliant at this kind of work but it was much easier – and more fun – for two people to struggle with it together. Terry and I would spend whole mornings immersed in this analytical and creative challenge. But it was time well spent: Wilson's opinions were interesting and original, and the end result was always a lively review.

Not so in the other case, that of the professor of politics Bernard Crick (later Sir Bernard). A review which Terry had commissioned from him and that it fell to me to edit contained such an impenetrable jumble of half-baked ideas that I took it home to enlist the help of my husband. John found it almost equally difficult to disentangle Crick's muddled thoughts – how did he come by his professorship? – and render them into clear English. I remember we spent the whole evening engaged in this thankless task. The end result was inevitably mediocre.

Later, I had two further encounters with Crick's writings. One concerned George Orwell. Orwell had stipulated in his will (he died in 1950) that no biography of him was to be written. His widow Sonia, who became a good friend of mine, kept numerous applicants at bay for many years, though various quasi-biographies were produced without the aid of private papers. Finally, the pressure became too great and Sonia felt that she could no longer go on saying no. She had, in any case, found just the person to do Orwell justice – Bernard Crick.

After much deliberating, John and I decided that it would be wrong to try to dissuade her from this choice on the basis of one book review – perhaps Crick would rise to the occasion. He didn't; at least not in Sonia's opinion. As soon as he showed her the first chapters of his book, she went into a deep depression, convinced that she had let Orwell down. Crick's biography, in the event, was quite well received. But several much better ones have appeared since.

Much later, in 2006, I stumbled across Crick again. I was teaching English to a group of adult immigrants from various countries who were eager to become British citizens. They were preparing to take the British citizenship test that had recently been introduced for all immigrants seeking to be naturalised, and they asked me to help them revise for it. I was very much in favour of such a test: it would give aspiring British subjects some background knowledge of the country's history and culture. So I was very interested to read the official manual on which the questions were based. It turned out to be an astonishingly ill-judged and inept booklet. It was full of statistics about the benefits system and about employment figures for women in different parts of the country. There was almost nothing about history or culture. I looked to see who had devised this document. Professor Crick, among others – say no more. (The test has since been changed to include more history.)

Literary editors, then and now, are continuously being importuned – by friends, by publishers, by bigwigs of all kinds – to review books they, or their nearest and dearest, have written. But Terry, whose mild and easy-going manner belied a remarkable toughness and a complete confidence in his own judgement, nearly always resisted. Anyone who tried to lean on him soon found that it was counter-productive. He was impervious to flattery and immune (or almost immune) to the corruption of friendship. He selected books for review entirely (or almost entirely) on the basis of their intrinsic merits. Indeed, Terry seemed to take pleasure in confounding the wishes and expectations of anyone who attempted to lobby him. This austere attitude to granting favours was unusual even in those days, half a century ago, when the public relations industry had only just begun its steady infiltration of the cultural world.

Terry applied the same kind of rigour to the process of editing. He had perfect literary pitch: if there was a single ill-chosen word or faulty rhythm or woolly argument in a piece of writing, he would immediately detect it and courteously insist that it be changed, however eminent the perpetrator. And he was averse to undue praise. Adverbs were routinely removed from the reviews. If a reviewer had written that a novel was 'exceedingly good', it would in most cases end up as 'good'. Adjectives, too, were always in danger of being chopped off. I remember an occasion when I foolishly showed Clive James the unedited typescript of a glowing review of his first book. James was ecstatic – only to discover that, when the review appeared on Sunday morning, it had been shorn of almost all favourable adjectives.

Terry had a perfectly valid explanation for this purge: it would look bad for the reputation of the book pages, and indeed for James himself, if the paper was seen to be heaping praise on its own contributors. Such an argument would be almost incomprehensible nowadays, when newspapers and magazines regard it as their duty to ensure that any book – however second-rate – written by someone they employ is greeted with applause.

A couple of years after starting work at the *Observer* I became pregnant. It would make no difference, I assured Terry – I would be back at the office in two or three weeks' time (maternity leave, as far as I was aware, had not yet been invented). I regarded myself as the kind of undomestic, unmaternal person who would have no problems combining full-time work and motherhood – with the help of a live-in au-pair girl. But I had not reckoned with the maternal instinct. As happens with most parents, all my priorities changed as soon as my baby was born. I had never before, I remember thinking, understood the real meaning of the word love. It was painful to tear myself away from my son even for an hour – the thought of going back to full-time work seemed an affront against nature.

Whatever feminists or sociologists may say, I am convinced that the feelings that come into being at the birth of a baby are stronger in the average mother than those of even the most doting father. At the same time, babies and young children are liable to turn to their mothers for love and comfort even when a devoted father is present. Indeed, the whole 'mothers and work' debate which has been raging for decades seems to me to play down the issues of the maternal instinct and the maternal role.

But I couldn't let Terry down at such short notice, so I went back to work about three weeks after the birth. It was a very stressful time. I used to come back home in the middle of the day to breastfeed, but the journey from Blackfriars station to West Hampstead took an age. Whenever the train was delayed, I used to weep with frustration on the platform – the cries of my hungry baby ringing in my head. After a month or two, I told Terry that I couldn't go on in this way. Luckily, literary editing is not so arduous that it can't be done without a full-time assistant – a little less time spent in the pub would make up the shortfall. Terry very generously suggested that I should stay in my job but come in just twice a week. It was the ideal solution and lasted for about seven years, till both my children went to school.

On one of these office days, a Friday in August 1968, I had one of the most nerve-wracking experiences of my working life. The book pages were all done, ready to go to press, and Terry had departed for a long weekend, leaving me on my own to finish off routine jobs in the office. In the early afternoon the phone rang. 'It's Wystan here, can I speak to Terry?' The line was crackly, the voice was deep and gravelly. Wystan, in my ignorance, was not a name I'd ever heard of. 'He's not here, I'm afraid. Can I help you?' 'I've written a short poem about Czechoslovakia, could you publish it in Sunday's paper?' The Soviet Union and its allies had just invaded that country, bringing the Prague Spring to a brutal end.

Normally I would have been dismissive of such a presumptuous demand and snapped that it was much too late for this Sunday's pages and that anyway poems had to be submitted for approval to the poetry editor. But there was a certain authority in this Wystan's tone that luckily made me hesitate, because he then rasped: 'It's Wystan Auden.' Oh my God, my mind reeled, W.H. Auden, my favourite poet. There was only one answer to his request: Yes.

Auden then proceeded to dictate the poem to me in his mid-Atlantic drawl. I could barely make out a single word. Usually in such situations one can pretend that one has understood at least some of what is being said, but that is not an option when taking down a poem for publication. To my intense embarrassment, I had to ask poor W.H. Auden to repeat and spell out every word of the poem, including 'the' and 'and'. I kept blaming the bad connection, but he must have thought I was an utter idiot. When this painful process was at last over, I rushed down to the 'stone' to persuade the printers, who were very busy working on news pages, that, for the sake of great poetry, they would have to remove one of the book reviews and reset the page. After some resistance, they agreed. When it was finally all done, I felt exhilarated. The poem is now included in Auden's collected works and in anthologies:

> *The Ogre does what ogres can,*
> *Deeds quite impossible for Man,*
> *But one prize is beyond his reach,*
> *The Ogre cannot master Speech.*
>
> *About a subjugated plain,*
> *Among its desperate and slain,*
> *The Ogre stalks with hands on hips,*
> *While drivel gushes from his lips.*

New York

Later that year, John was invited to America, to be a visiting professor at Rutgers University – the state university of New Jersey – for one term. As Rutgers is only about 30 minutes by train from Manhattan, we thought that this was an unmissable opportunity to live in New York for a few months. Terry agreed to keep my job open.

From the moment we landed at Kennedy Airport with our two small infants – aged three and one and a half – I was enraptured. Nothing was as I had expected. For a start, New York's attitude to children. Every official we dealt with at the airport – customs officers, passport controllers, baggage handlers – ushered us through with amiable smiles and good-natured jokes. This child-friendliness continued wherever we went in the city, and throughout our stay. Restaurants provided high-chairs and special menus; shop assistants, even in deluxe stores such as Saks, Fifth Avenue, made a fuss of the children, taking time off to show them colourful items; commuters helped to lift pushchairs up and down stairs at subway stations.

Once I discovered how helpful New Yorkers were, I explored much of Manhattan on buses, even riding all the way to Harlem, which I had been warned could be dangerous. I found nothing but genuine warmth and consideration, especially from bus conductresses, who all seemed to have bits of candy hidden in one of their pockets.

We had rented a small two-bedroom apartment in a large residential hotel on the Upper West Side. It was slightly seedy but very convenient. On its ground floor there was a coffee shop, and this was my second revelation. It was a coffee shop unlike anything that existed in England at the time. To begin with, it was open at all hours of the day and night. Then, if you ordered a cup of coffee, it would be refilled as often as you liked, for the same price. What's more, the coffee was always fresh. You could order as much or as little food as you wanted. Cottage cheese salad, cinnamon toast, scrambled eggs, prawn cocktail, fresh melon slices – to name some of my favourites – were available throughout the day at very reasonable prices. You could, if you wished, have breakfast at dinner time. Meanwhile, in England, undrinkable coffee, egg and chips, limp lettuce leaves and tinned pineapple with lumpy custard were the order of the day.

New York was full of such magical eateries but the one attached to our hotel seemed to us the greatest. I spent many hours there, especially during the day, when John was at Rutgers. The elderly waitress, who never seemed to sleep and always wore a red hairband, became a friend.

Other surprises included the city's museums which, like its coffee shops, were much more welcoming than English ones. England has since then more than caught up. But in those days American museums were brighter and more imaginatively laid out – and information about the artworks was much more accessible.

I spent much of my time in New York writing stories for young children – putting on paper, that is, stories that I'd been telling my three-year-old son at bedtime. One reason for trying my hand at this genre was that I'd been looking, while still at the office in London, at dozens of new children's books. I'd found that many of them were plot-less and pointless. What's more, they were often illustrated with highly stylised, even abstract, pictures, which seemed to me quite unsuitable for the very young. Children enjoy the pleasures of recognition and they like action. These works might well put them off the whole idea of books. Perhaps I could do better.

I can't now remember much about my own stories, except that they had a great deal of plot and involved burglars, policemen and intelligent dogs, with a few witches and ogres thrown in. And children, of course. I sent a collection of them – it was called Tommy and his Terrible Tantrums – to one publisher after another. They all turned it down. The mixture of realism and magic in these stories, the publishers all agreed, didn't really work. They were probably right and I didn't much mind. My son, at any rate, very much appreciated my efforts.

1968 was the year of student demonstrations in many parts of the world, most famously the *évènements* in Paris but also the protests at New York's Columbia University. Strikes, blockades and occupations of buildings had closed down Columbia for almost a week. The students were protesting, at least ostensibly, against the war in Vietnam, against racism, against the university's involvement with weapons research. In the end the police had been summoned. This had occurred in April, before we arrived, but the academic world was still in shock. One of the people who had mediated between the students and the Columbia administrators was the renowned literary critic Lionel Trilling, who had been a professor of English literature at Columbia since 1939. He had been horrified by the destructiveness of the students and equally appalled by the brute force of the police.

John was a great admirer of Lionel Trilling and had at various times been in correspondence with him; they had very similar views about the overly academic approach to the teaching of literature in universities. Soon after we arrived in New York, he and his wife Diana invited us to lunch in their flat near the university. The Trillings were the undisputed high priests of New York's intellectual world. He had written several influential books but had made his name with *The Liberal Imagination*, a brilliant collection of cultural essays, which became a surprise best-seller. She was also a prolific literary and social critic, whose themes included the assassination of President Kennedy and the significance of Marilyn Monroe.

We liked them immediately; both of them were warm and humorous, though in every other respect their characters could not have been more unalike. Lionel was modest and self-deprecating, calm, measured and mild – and perhaps a bit vain; Diana, who was not at all vain, was edgy and confrontational, and so brimming with cultural theories – some of them, it seemed to me, quite wrong-headed – that one felt she might boil over at any moment.

The eminent literary critic Lionel
Trilling in 1970

The Trillings were more than old enough to be our

parents and they took us up in something of a parental spirit. We were often invited to their flat, where they would acquaint us with the marital difficulties of various of their academic friends and neighbours. Diana, I recall, was convinced that every other woman was a lesbian; she was astonished when I told her that no one had ever made advances at me in any ladies' lavatory. But our conversations always circled back to the student protests, their causes and consequences. Both Trillings believed that the students were not really motivated by the issues; rather, they were seeking the gratification of feeling that they were at the centre of politics. In any event, the Trillings thought, the issues were the responsibility of the government, not of the university; so the students were attacking the wrong place and the wrong people.

Lionel was both a firm liberal and an unwavering anti-communist. He wrote indirectly about political themes, but he was not an overtly political writer. He had, however, exerted a profound influence on two former students who now represented opposing political factions in New York intellectual life. In one corner was Norman Podhoretz, the editor of the right-leaning, neo-conservative Jewish magazine *Commentary*; in the other, was Jason Epstein, who was the power behind the throne at the left-leaning *New York Review of Books*, described by Tom Wolfe as 'the chief theoretical organ of Radical Chic'. (The *NYRB* had been launched during the New York newspaper strike of 1963.)

Both sides of this divide wanted to claim their guru as a sympathiser, but Trilling did not wish to be identified with either camp or indeed to be slotted into any category at all. In a memoir of their marriage that Diana wrote after his death, she states firmly that her husband would never have embraced neo-conservatism. 'Nothing in his thought supports sectarianism,' she wrote. This led one of her friends to claim that she was 'moving Lionel's coffin to the left, lest the neo-conservatives take possession of it.'

John, who was a regular contributor both to the *New York Review of Books* and to *Commentary* magazine, equally resisted being enlisted by either side. But, like Trilling, he was deeply opposed to the anti-American orthodoxies of the Left.

Two or three years after we'd returned from New York, the Trillings came for a short visit to London. They hated hotels, so we invited them to stay at our house. We took great trouble to make everything as comfortable as possible, to the point of moving out of our own bedroom and into a spare room in the attic. When they arrived, the Trillings were in high spirits and we all had a welcoming tea party in our sitting room. My daughter Susanna, a humorous child who was then four years old, was perched happily on Lionel's knee munching biscuits. Suddenly, during a lull in the conversation, she turned to John. 'Daddy', she demanded in a clear, piping voice, 'why did you say that you don't you like Lionel?' John had never said anything of the kind. He adored Lionel.

A terrible hush descended. John and I were beside ourselves with embarrassment. The Trillings looked crestfallen. Out of the mouths of babes... they must have thought. We tried as hard as we could to convince them that there was not an iota of truth in this remark, that it was indeed the opposite of the truth, that Susanna simply thought it was a funny thing to say. The Trillings politely insisted that we were making too much of the incident. But, being Freudians, they probably thought that there had to be some subconscious memory that had prompted Susanna's question. Our friendship survived, but it was never the same.

Back to the *Observer*

By the time I returned to full-time work in the 70s, I had completed a long apprenticeship in literary editing. Terry was already immersed in Proust, so he was pleased to leave me to make some of the decisions about what books should be reviewed. People have often asked me how on earth it's possible, from all those dozens of titles, to make an informed choice. In fact it is much easier than it seems: knowing whether a book is good from reading a few pages may be difficult, but there's not much problem discerning when it's bad. That eliminates about half of the books that are sent in. Nevertheless, the system is undoubtedly unfair: many promising authors are bound to be excluded, and inevitably preference has to be given to well-known ones.

More novels were reviewed in those days than now. Instead of writing about them singly, they were assessed in 'round-ups' consisting of four or five titles. Our method of selection when it came to unfamiliar fiction writers might be regarded as somewhat frivolous, though I would dispute this. It was based on physiognomy. It's true that you can't judge a book by its cover, but you can tell quite a lot about it from the author's photograph on the dust jacket. Not necessarily from his or her features, but from poses, expressions, hairstyles and clothes. Novelists with bushy beards or long sideburns fared badly with Terry and me.

It was at around this time that I started doing lengthy interviews for the paper, mainly with authors, but also with politicians. I can't now remember how this happened but I had tried my hand at fiction reviewing and failed – it seems to me one of the most difficult forms of writing. Interviewing is much easier, particularly in the 'question-and-answer' format in which it used to be done. Even so, the interviews took me a great deal of time and effort. One reason for this was a lack of professionalism: I spent much too long talking to the interviewees, so that when I got home I found that I had recorded 20,000 words, or more, which had to be boiled down to 4000 or less. John frequently helped me with this task.

Nowadays, interviews are more often than not controlled by PR people, who have an iron grip on the whole procedure. They impose strict conditions on anyone who wants to talk to their charges: the interview can last so many minutes; it must be built around the person's forthcoming work; it has to steer clear of various aspects of his or her background. The resulting articles – quasi plugs – are usually printed before the merits or demerits of the interviewee's work have even been ascertained.

This was not the case when I worked at the *Observer*. Quite the reverse. PRs were ignored and the interviewees were chosen on the basis of recognised achievement. The 'peg' would often be an anniversary or birthday. I interviewed John le Carré and Harold Pinter* on their 50th birthdays, Anthony Powell* at 80 and A.J. Ayer at 70; I interviewed, among others, the poet Philip Larkin* and the painter Francis Bacon* for no particular reason at all. I had a great advantage in being married to John, who had become a successful author: it gave me access to distinguished writers who might otherwise not grant interviews to journalists. Journalists, then as now, were not held in high esteem – talking to them was likely to result in misrepresentations and distortions.

My most dramatic interview was with Stalin's daughter, Svetlana (who died in 2011). It was dramatic in two senses. First, because the idea of a murderous tyrant's daughter actually coming to lunch at my house -- such was the plan – seemed bizarre in the extreme. I went around for days accosting everyone I met: 'Guess who's coming for lunch with me next week – yes, can you believe it? Stalin's daughter!' But it was also dramatic because in the course of writing up the interview, we developed quite an intense relationship, which ended on a somewhat sour note.

Svetlana had defected from the Soviet Union in 1967, leaving her two eldest children behind. At a hugely publicised press conference in New York, she had denounced her father and all his works. She had spent sixteen years

* *These interviews are reproduced in full at the back of this book.*

in the US, where she had married and divorced an American (her third husband), and had then moved to England with her young daughter from that marriage. Now, in 1984, she had completely changed her mind about the West and was on the brink of returning to the Soviet Union. Though Glasnost had not yet arrived, she sensed its approach.

I took to Svetlana as soon as she came through the front door. She was an attractive woman, neatly dressed, polite and forthright. She was also formidably intelligent and articulate, despite her imperfect English. Our interview went well, though she refused to say anything about Stalin (or rather, she mentioned him once: 'Over me my father's shadow hovers, no matter what I do or say.') What she mainly wanted to talk about was the threat of nuclear war. All our attitudes to the USSR and the USA, she believed, were obsolete. She had been 'blinded by admiration of the Free World'; but 'what I did not realise seventeen years ago was how similar the two superpowers are.'

After our meeting, and before the publication of the interview, she wrote me a whole series of densely typed, impassioned letters. The first began: 'Thank you for your hospitality. Your house is very pleasant (to my taste) and the salad was very good indeed... On my way home, and this morning, I feel that I missed a few important points in our conversation...' One letter consisted of seven A4 pages (with a handwritten postscript: 'Enough now, or I'm going to have a heart attack').

In all the letters, she was anxious to explain how her experiences in the US, where she was patronised and exploited – by the CIA, by her publishers, by her lawyers – and where she was kept under constant surveillance, had led her to change her views. 'We must all now turn to LOVE [Svetlana's letters were full of capitals and under-linings] and reject all and everybody who is still calling us to HATRED… PLEASE do not think that I had some personal bad experiences in USA and THEREFORE I talk now about how they are both alike… I had, and I will have my bad experiences everywhere – this is my lot and luckily I do know that…'

When I finally showed her the text of our interview, into which I had inserted some parts of her letters (the interview was well over 3000 words long), Svetlana was extremely appreciative and grateful – I had not distorted or misrepresented her views, she said. She was particu-larly pleased with the part about her mother, Nadya Alliluyeva, who killed herself when Svetlana was a child, and whose suicide had been hushed up.

After the publication of the interview, however, Svetlana became increasingly agitated. For a start, she objected strongly to the photograph (by the *Observer*'s well-known photographer Jane Bown): 'that pitiful (and ugly) photo'; she also disliked the headline ('Between Two Worlds'): 'poor old lady between the two worlds and all alone…' And she worried that she would be quoted out of context and be made to look like a peacenik or a CND supporter.

A few days later, her anger turned against me: 'I am

outraged with the photo – as any woman would be – from that angle even Liz Taylor would look ugly. But you are telling me that the picture is nice. Please, stop talking to me as if I am a little girl... Thank you for letting me get some of my views to the public. But together with this [the photo], the public got the wrong impression of my supposed loneliness – and now ladies and gents are pushing to be friends. How sickening. It always impresses me how secure, protected, hidden and "above it all" YOU, media people are: you know how to guard yourselves from any possible distortions... You do not understand. Freedom is inside... you do not understand that because your talk was all about democracy, Gulag, cliché things.'

So our relationship deteriorated. This process had already started when, just before the interview was published, I had declined an invitation to visit her in Cambridge, where she was living – I was simply too busy at the time. But I always liked her. Though her experiences in America (moving 'from one cage to another') had clearly warped her judgement about life in the West, it is difficult to imagine that anyone else would have reacted very differently. Yes, she was needy and volatile – which was hardly surprising – but she was at the same time honest, and proud – she hated the thought that anyone might pity her. Her grievances about the photograph and even about the headline, and certainly about the media, were not unjustified.

Also, she was generous-hearted. In her last letter to me she quotes a 'special' friend in Moscow, someone who had gone through 'all the circles of hell'. He told her that he divided all human beings into two large categories: 'the harmless; and those who are harmful. Nothing else mattered'. 'You' she wrote 'certainly are among the harmless... Making an interview with someone you've never met is always a difficult thing.' She was a remarkable woman – all the more so, of course, when you consider her extraordinary and tragic background.

When, in 1981, the post of woman's editor of the *Observer* fell vacant, I applied for it and got it. I was now my own boss and indeed the boss of several others. The women's section was twice the size of the book section – four broadsheet pages – and my job was to think up ideas and commission articles that would be of special interest to women readers. As far as I was concerned, that included all human life, with a few possible exceptions such as mechanical engineering. But of course we (my deputy and I) focused mainly on traditional female concerns: education, adultery, domestic help, eating disorders and so on. It was a much more demanding job than literary editing: the articles we commissioned often didn't work out.

Journalists are very lucky when it comes to perks (perquisites). In my previous job I had been able to obtain almost any book I wanted for free. Now I was the recipient of vast numbers of packages – lipsticks, tights, toilet bags, gloves, napkins, shampoos, anti-wrinkle creams – free samples of new products from manufacturers. In the US journalists are not allowed to accept such 'bribes', but there are no similar prohibitions in England. These goodies were of course shared out among the staff, though I always kept the latest 'anti-ageing' products for myself – I was now in my early forties.

One of our four pages was given over to fashion. I had not realised quite what a sealed-off, self-important world the fashion industry was, full of rules, rituals and rankings. One of my first tasks as woman's editor had been to appoint a new fashion editor. I chose the one – from among dozens of applicants – who seemed to me the least one-track-minded. This she may have been, but my candidate nevertheless turned out to be totally in thrall to voguish values – which did not include ordinary clothes. When I suggested to her that it might be a good idea occasionally to devote the fashion page to everyday garments such as might be obtained at Marks and Spencer or John Lewis, she threw a hissy fit. To do such a thing, she wailed, would make her a laughing stock among her rivals on other newspapers and magazines. She even ran off to cry on the editor's shoulder, where she received a warm welcome. This was not surprising: she was a blonde with large breasts: attributes which were of overriding interest to Donald Trelford, who had taken over as editor from David Astor in 1975.

One day – I had been woman's editor for four years – I was asked to go to the editor's office. Could I try, he asked me, to make the women's pages more raunchy. 'Raunchy?' What a horrible word. No I couldn't. I resigned there and then, bringing my career at the *Observer* to an abrupt end. Actually, Trelford had a point. On the previous Sunday I had published, against my better judgement, a very unraunchy, esoteric article about the Marxist art critic and novelist John Berger. It was totally unsuitable for women's pages and I had published it for entirely unprofessional reasons: in order not to upset its author, whom I liked, and who had taken a great deal of time and trouble to write it.

After leaving the *Observer*, I did a few further interviews, most memorably with one of Nazi Germany's 'good Germans' (it was published in the *Sunday Times*). Axel von dem Busche, an army officer, was a member of an old aristocratic family (his mother was Danish) who, in 1943, had single-handedly attempted to assassinate Hitler. It was a suicide mission. The top-secret plan – in which he had been encouraged and helped by some of the people later involved in the July plot of 1944 – required von dem Busche to act as a male model for new military uniforms which were to be shown to Hitler for his approval. When he got near enough, he was to throw himself at the Fuehrer and detonate a bomb hidden in his pocket.

It never happened. The train that was delivering the uniforms was itself bombed. Von dem Busche went back to the front, where one of his legs was blown off. He spent the rest of the war in hospital, which is how he came to escape the savage retribution meted out by Hitler, after the failure of the July plot, to anyone who had any connection with the plotters.

This brave man was impelled to make his heroic attempt by one specific event. In 1942, in the Ukraine, he had witnessed a mile-long queue of naked Jewish men, women and children being made to lie down in holes in the ground which they had themselves been forced to dig – and then being shot by the SS.

Unlike so many Germans – and others – von dem Busche couldn't live with the knowledge that such depravity was taking place without fighting against it. Inevitably, my conversation with him made me think about the fate of my maternal grandparents. A similar end, in all probability, had befallen them.

Social Life

During the two decades in which I worked at the *Observer*, John (who became editor of the *Times Literary Supplement* in 1974) and I got to know many writers and politicians and were invited to numerous book launches and dinner parties. But it was mainly due to one man that we enjoyed what could almost be described as a 'glittering' social life: the publisher George Weidenfeld. George – now in his nineties – is one of the most imaginative and resourceful men of his generation. Our friendship with him enhanced not just our social life but the quality of our life generally: we met many people who would become lifelong friends directly or indirectly through George.

In those days George gave countless dinner parties (he still, today, gives many more than most people). Indeed, his elegant literary and political gatherings are often compared to the fashionable Parisian salons of the eighteenth and nineteenth centuries. George saw himself as a kind of impresario of human connections: he liked bringing together piano players and scientists, house-wives and philosophers, novelists and economists. His parties – they were usually given in honour of one of his authors – typically started as formal dinners for about twenty people and ended as stand-up gatherings, when a stream of after-dinner guests arrived. George was very particular about who came to his soirées – his was at no time an open house.

My first experience of one of these evenings was an embarrassing non-event. I had barely met George – his contact had been mainly with John, whose forthcoming book *The Rise and Fall of the Man of Letters* he was soon to publish – when I found myself standing next to him at a very crowded, noisy party. It was being held at the house of the journalist Nick Tomalin and his wife Claire, later to become a distinguished biographer, but at that point a full-time mother of small children. George put one of his arms around my shoulders and the other round the shoulders of a tough-looking young woman from New York. 'Could you both come for dinner at my house next Thursday,' he requested, 'with your husbands?' I could only just hear him above the din. We both nodded enthusiastic assent.

When we got home after the party, I informed John about this invitation. Was it to be taken seriously, or was it just the kind of friendly but meaningless suggestion that George might be in the habit of making when he met young women at parties? Or perhaps he was tipsy? We pondered the matter and decided that he couldn't really have meant it and that, if he had, he or his secretary would surely phone to confirm. It would be mortifying, we felt, to arrive at his home and find that there was no party in progress or, if there was, that we weren't expected.

When Thursday arrived we went to bed early as we often did at that time since I was pregnant with my second child. Shortly after 9pm the phone rang. 'Where are you? My guests are all waiting for their dinner.' Calamity. It was too late to get dressed and drive across London – we lived in West Hampstead, George at that time in Knightsbridge. So sorry, we stammered, it was a misunderstanding. We immediately composed a grovelling letter of apology and delivered it by hand the following morning.

This social blunder taught us two things about George: that he knew exactly what he was doing, and that he was a teetotaller. (The New York lady, who was to become Lady Harlech, had, I learned later, attended.) Nevertheless, George soon asked us again and we gradually became part of a circle of close friends whom he regularly invited to gatherings large and small. Though George was a 'networker' (as it would now be called) on a global scale, he also liked to include some friendly, familiar faces in among his other guests. As a result, the people I have found myself sitting around the same table as – though not necessarily exchanging words with – include Harold Wilson, Moshe Dayan, James Mason, Henry Kissinger, Helmut Kohl, Peter Ustinov, 'Lady Bird' Johnson, Edward Heath, Princess Firyal of Jordan, Alfred Brendel, Lauren Bacall, Alec Guinness, Saul Bellow, Sam Spiegel,

Giovanni Agnelli, Angela Merkel, Gore Vidal, Shimon Peres and various descendants of Richard Wagner. To name but some.

Towards the end of many of these dinners, George would tap on his glass (from which he only drank apple juice) and introduce a general conversation on some topic of the day: How good a prime minister had Mrs Thatcher been? Should we join the euro? What will be the consequences for Israel of the invasion of Iraq? He would ask guests who were experts in the relevant field to give their views, and this would often lead to very instructive discussions.

Such gatherings, where everyone, including oneself, is so anxious to please and to impress, afford ideal opportunities for observing the 'human comedy'. John and I would often, on our way home, enjoy comparing notes on the social intercourse we had witnessed at these events as much as the events themselves.

When I asked George, in an interview I did with him for the *Observer* in the early 1980s, about his propensity for party-giving, this was his reply: 'I've always preferred being a host to a guest. I like conviviality, perhaps because I was an only child. I felt when I was younger an excitement, a febrile excitement, in going into a room and hearing the noise of chatter and conversation. And I've always had the almost childish desire to bring people together: I want all my friends to like each other... On the other hand, I can't bear being talked about as a host. Entertaining is of course very much a secondary activity, an accessory to my work. As a publisher, I need continuing and sustained contact with a large variety of people and worlds; and since I travel a great deal I receive a large amount of hospitality which I feel I have to repay. I think that many people don't realise what it means to be excessively energetic. If they hear of me as a party-giver, they assume that that is where most of my energy goes.'

George had escaped from Nazi-occupied Vienna in 1938, at the age of nineteen, and arrived in England with a small suitcase and a postal order for 16 shillings and sixpence (about £20 today). With the help of the British Fund for Refugees, he found lodgings with a family of Plymouth Brethren who treated him as one of the family. Though he had been educated to a very high academic level – he spoke fluent French and Italian as well as his native German – George knew very little English and had to learn it more or less from scratch, which he very quickly did. He now speaks it with Nabokovian virtuosity.

Within a year of arriving, before he was even twenty, he applied for and, despite stiff competition, was offered a job with the BBC's new wartime monitoring service. 'The BBC was everything to me,' he told me, 'my finishing school, a window onto English life, a road to the future.'

George is an accomplished mimic. His renderings of various eccentric Austrian academics are as funny as anything I have ever heard. Not long after he joined the BBC, he became known for the inspired imitations of the speeches of Hitler and Mussolini with which he enter- tained colleagues in the canteen. This talent was soon to prove invaluable on a prime-time BBC programme called

The Shadow of the Swastika. It was a programme that regularly broadcast the authentic voice of Hitler. One evening the recording of a Hitler speech failed to arrive. What to do? Luckily, someone recalled the canteen performances of an enthusiastic young Austrian. George was hurriedly summoned for an audition – and was then asked to stand in. As a result, a large BBC audience, which believed that it was hearing the voice of Hitler, was in fact listening to the youthful George Weidenfeld. (In later years, George was occasionally persuaded to launch into one of these hilarious tirades – they sounded indistinguishable from the originals.)

By the time John and I got to know him, George had become a formidable publisher. Together with his partner Nigel Nicolson, he had set up one of the most enterprising publishing houses in England. But it had not been done without a great deal of struggle or without incurring quite a bit of hostility. He was regarded by some rivals as an interloper who had introduced sharp business practices into the gentlemanly old world of English publishing; or as a social-climbing parvenu insinuating his way into the British establishment.

These assessments were based on envy or on anti-Semitism. No doubt George has at some points behaved in a ruthlessly opportunistic way: so do most self-made men at the outset of their careers in a competitive business. But his success in the world of publishing is entirely based on his inspirational ideas for interesting and important new books. Moreover, he is a great deal more cultivated than his critics – certainly than various old-style English publishers whom I've come across. George is immensely knowledgeable, a walking Wikipedia, not just of history and current affairs, but of music, art and European literature; he can quote reams of Goethe. At the same time, he can tell you the life stories of hundreds of living people including, unlike Wikipedia, an account of their love lives. Indeed, I have often wondered how George has managed to become so erudite, given his frenetically active business and social life. (Not to mention his amorous pursuits). The answer is energy – and a marvellous memory.

George's achievements have long ago silenced all doubters. Apart from publishing, he has launched a whole range of programmes, most of them designed to increase mutual understanding between people of different nations, cultures and religions. He has inaugurated a series of Weidenfeld lectures and scholarships for foreign students at Oxford University and elsewhere. And he has received high honours and awards from numerous countries.

In his autobiography, which came out in 1994, George wrote: 'My friendship with both of them [John and me] runs like a thread through the last 30 years. In their different ways they have been indispensable companions.' This still holds true for me today, and it held true for John until the day of his death in 2011.

Another figure who, in those days, gave dinner parties for writers and artists, though on a much smaller, more domestic scale, was Sonia Orwell, the widow of George Orwell. Sonia was not universally liked. She was certainly not liked by me at our first meeting. John knew her before we were married and he arranged, soon afterwards, for the three of us to go out for a meal. Sonia was then in her late forties, a good-looking, somewhat blowsy blonde who had clearly been extremely pretty in her younger days. She smoked heavily and had a correspondingly husky voice.

As soon as we were seated at our table, she and John launched into a non-stop exchange of gossip. They talked about people I didn't know, books I hadn't read, events I hadn't been to. Neither of them made the slightest attempt to draw me into the conversation, nor did Sonia ask me a single question about myself. She was a heavy drinker, and after a few glasses of wine she started peppering her conversation with French phrases and *mots justes* (she was an ardent Francophile), while her voice grew louder and more overbearing, provoking stares from other diners. For me, it was an evening from hell.

As soon as dinner was over and we got into our car (in those days you could park freely outside more or less any London restaurant), I began berating John for his appallingly insensitive and tactless behaviour – unacceptable in any husband, let alone a new one. I became more and more incensed and finally did something suicidally reckless: I snatched off John's glasses – he was driving – and threw them out of the window and into the traffic. John was extremely short-sighted – at two metres he wouldn't have known a lamp-post from a pedestrian. I can't now remember how we got home. John must have had a spare pair in the glove compartment.

Though I mainly blamed John for this episode, it certainly revealed some of the less appealing aspects of Sonia's character. She was well known, it turned out, for causing rifts and tensions in the marriages of friends: she would focus entirely on one partner while ignoring the other. Perhaps this was unconscious. When, a few years later, she took a bit of a shine to me – she was prone to infatuations with women as well as men – she started behaving as though John didn't exist. And she singled out my small son Tom, whom she adored, showering him with presents, while ignoring my daughter.

I soon discovered, though, that Sonia had redeeming qualities that outweighed all her flaws. She was high-spirited and fearless; she had great warmth and generosity; and she was genuinely enthusiastic and discerning about literature. To people who didn't know her she may have seemed pretentious or foolish, but she was in fact highly intelligent. Yes, she was an intellectual snob – but that's hardly much of a crime.

Thinking about Sonia now, I realise that she must have been deeply unhappy even in the late 60s and early 70s, when I was getting to know her, and before she sank into the depression that consumed her before her death in 1980. I was only dimly aware of this at the time, because she was always so ebullient.

Sonia had been born in India in 1918, into a colonial family, and educated at an English convent. She had found both these facets of her background unbearably stifling and had escaped from them by plunging into London's bohemian and literary life. First, in the late 1930s, she became an artists' model for the Euston Road Set, a group of realist painters who either taught or studied at the School of Painting located there. She befriended many artists including the young Lucian Freud and Francis Bacon – and earned the title of 'Euston Road Venus'.

Sonia Orwell, literary hostess and widow of George

A year or two later, she achieved her ambition of entering into the literary world. She became assistant to the editor of the influential magazine *Horizon*, Cyril Connolly. *Horizon* ran from 1940 to 1949 and offered an outlet – one of the very few during that period – for promising writers, several of them spotted by Sonia. It was at *Horizon* that she met many of the leading authors of the period, among them T.S. Eliot, W.H. Auden, Evelyn Waugh, Anthony Powell, Stephen Spender – and George Orwell.

Sonia married George Orwell when he was on his deathbed in London's University College Hospital. According to his close friend the journalist Malcolm

Muggeridge, 'she represented everything he [Orwell] had always longed for; she was beautiful, and in a generous, luxuriant way; gifted socially, the familiar of writers and painters.' For the wedding, Orwell wore a mauve smoking jacket over his pyjamas, bought for him by Anthony Powell.

For a few weeks after the wedding, Orwell's condition seemed to improve. He was full of projects about the books he was going to write; one, for example, about anti-British sentiment in the United States. The couple planned soon to fly to a sanatorium in Switzerland, where it was hoped that Orwell would be cured. But it was not to be. He died the day before they were due to leave. 'Sonia came to see us the same evening,' remembers Muggeridge. 'She cried and cried. I will always love her for her true tears on that occasion.' So much for cynics who claim that she married Orwell simply because he had become a famous writer.

Sonia married again, briefly and unhappily, and then resumed her life in literary London as, among other things, a hostess. She took immense trouble to make her dinner parties a success. She was an excellent cook – she had been a friend of the cookery writer Elizabeth David – and she travelled all round London to find the best ingredients for her exotic *spécialités de la maison*.

Unfortunately, the evenings too often ended in some kind of row. It only took two glasses of wine to make Sonia tipsy, at which point she would launch into a tirade about the superiority of all things French to all things English, particularly of French intellectuals to English intellectuals, some of whom were sitting around her table.

But the two dinners I most clearly remember were the opposite of rowdy. At the first, the main guests were the American poet Robert Lowell and the writer Caroline Blackwood, who were newly married. They were madly in love. So much so that he had felt compelled to leave his wife of 23 years (the American writer Elizabeth Hardwick) and make his home in England. Caroline, a long-standing friend of Sonia's, had, in her twenties, been briefly married to – and famously painted by – Lucian Freud. She was very beautiful. Throughout the dinner they gazed deeply into each other's eyes – hers were huge and pale blue – while Lowell expounded on the merits of mature love.

He, at this point, was in his early fifties, Caroline in her early forties. He told us (there were six or eight people around the table) that Shakespeare, more than any other writer, had truly understood – as he showed in *Anthony and Cleopatra* and elsewhere – that true love, the fusion of sexual and spiritual passion, was only realisable when one had passed one's youth. Before that ('My salad days, when I was green in judgement, cold in blood'), people were still floundering around learning about themselves and about other people. Human beings, Lowell said, came into full flower in middle age – or words to that effect. We all agreed. It was an enthralling dinner party.

The other occasion, though similar in content, was less elevated in style. In this case Lucian Freud, also now middle-aged, arrived with a young woman with whom he was clearly smitten. Like Lowell, he focused single-mindedly on his partner throughout the evening. But instead of fascinating reflections on the nature of romantic love, these lovers indulged in a non-stop stream of amorous whispering and giggling. Unlike the Lowells, they were seated next to each other. It was difficult to know where to look. The couple seemed wholly unconcerned that they made conversation for others extremely difficult. But their behaviour offered an illuminating glimpse into Lucian Freud's anarchic personality.

The one time I met W.H. Auden was also at one of Sonia's dinners. Because he was obsessive about punctuality, the evening was organised with military precision. Sonia commanded us to arrive not a minute later than 6.30pm, when Auden was due for his first martini. Dinner would start on the dot of 7pm and end at 9 o'clock sharp, just before the poet's bedtime. His entire day, Sonia told me, ran according to a strict timetable. I was rather nervous about meeting this great man: he was known, among other things, as a brilliant conversationalist.

On this occasion, though, he was very quiet, even shy, and very endearing. He looked like a large, abandoned teddy bear. There were very few of us around the table because he didn't like large gatherings, but even so he spoke only when someone asked him a question. I didn't ask him any questions, though I was seated next to him; nor did I tell him that I was the idiot to whom he had dictated his poem about the crushing of the Prague Spring. He didn't seem much interested in anything except his food. What I didn't realise at the time was that he was already ill. He would die two years later, in 1973, at the age of 66.

Channel Four television

When I left the *Observer*, everyone told me that I would be sure to find another job right away – people would be falling over themselves to offer me one. I thought this very unlikely but it turned out to be even less true than I anticipated. All my applications for jobs were either turned down or ignored, so were letters and CVs I sent to various editors of papers and magazines. The furthest I got was to be interviewed for the job of assistant features editor of *Harpers and Queen* fashion magazine. But no, they wanted someone younger. This state of affairs continued for two years.

I remember lamenting with a friend, Suzanne Lowry, who was in a similar position – she had been woman's editor at both the *Observer* and the *Sunday Times* – that nobody wanted to employ women in their forties, at least in journalism. Employers, both male and female, favoured pliable younger women: older ones with experience were likely to be opinionated and bossy. We were unemployable. This view turned out to be unduly pessimistic. Both of us were eventually appointed to senior positions at the *Daily Telegraph*, a less sexist and ageist publication than its more fashionable rivals.

Like buses, jobs, after a long wait, often arrive in pairs. At the beginning of 1986, I was offered an exciting, albeit part-time, job by Jeremy Isaacs. He had been chief executive of Channel Four since its launch in 1981 and had, more than anyone, given the new channel its distinctive character. Now he had conceived the typically bold – not to say highbrow – idea of broadcasting a short, spoken, weekly book review. It was to go out every Friday, straight after the Channel Four news at 7.50pm; it was to last four minutes. Would I consider editing it? Consider? I couldn't believe my luck.

It was, in fact, more a freelance assignment than a job. Once it was up and running, it involved about half a day's work a week. But this half-day couldn't have been more engrossing. For one thing, I was delighted to enter what I saw as the glamorous world of television, even though I was only dipping a toe into it. Bookish people are usually not thought of as television enthusiasts, but that's just what John and I were. We were hooked on a whole raft of soap operas, and we were tireless followers of news bulletins and current affairs programmes. Indeed, to the consternation of some of our friends, we liked having the television on in the background while we did other things, including reading.

So when I was allotted a corner of an office at the ITN studios in Wells Street (in central London) where the Channel Four news and its four-minute sequel were broadcast, I felt I had arrived at the epicentre of contemporary life.

The person whose office I shared was an exceptionally clever and humorous young woman in her twenties, Fiona Maddocks (she is now the chief music critic of the *Observer*), who became a close friend. She had been part of the original team which set up Channel Four and was in charge of one of its most innovative and controversial programmes: *Comment*. The purpose of this programme was to provide a platform for ordinary people who wanted to make a strong point about a particular issue. These short monologues (a kind of early version of blogging, which often had to be completely rewritten by Fiona) went out four times a week, from Mondays to Thursdays, and filled the same slot, after the Channel Four news, as the new book programme would fill on Fridays. So Fiona had a great deal of experience in this form of broadcasting and she was deputed to show me how it was done.

But first I had to set up a miniature literary department from scratch and to decide on the kind of books and reviewers that should appear on *Book Choice*, as the programme was to be called. In doing this, I was left entirely to my own devices. I started by informing all the main British publishers about this new venture. Naturally they, and their authors, were delighted by the additional opportunity to gain publicity, and they were eager to send me any books I asked for. Next I decided that it would be more fun (though also more of a headache) not to use regular reviewers, but to commission a different person every week. (Since this programme ran for almost four years, I did, along the way, ask some of the best contributors two or three times.) I also thought that it would be more interesting to choose, whenever possible, contributors whose faces were unfamiliar to television audiences – writers and academics of whom they might have heard, but had not seen. I knew that I would need to edit ruthlessly any reviews that were not sufficiently conversational in tone: the difference between the written and the spoken word is much greater than people realise.

Meanwhile, I was rather doubtful about the whole idea of a spoken review. 'Talking heads' (when the heads belong to accomplished people, that is) are generally undervalued by programme makers, it has always seemed to me. But literary criticism, more than most forms of writing, is intended to be read, rather than 'talked'. Book reviews are not usually very dramatic. With their cultural allusions and fine distinctions, they are not designed for easy listening – unless, of course, they are savage attacks. Moreover, the kind of people who are good at book reviewing are not necessarily good at projecting themselves in public. Perhaps everyone I asked would refuse to do it. This little programme, I feared, might end in total fiasco.

As it turned out, *Book Choice* was not a fiasco, but nor was it a roaring success. Nearly everybody, I discovered, wanted to appear on television, so I needn't have worried on that score. But there was no way of knowing in advance who would and who wouldn't be good at it. Auditioning writers and academics in order to find out how well they could read aloud was out of the question, and there was no time for rehearsal. Consequently, though the scripts themselves were always interesting, the actual readings were sometimes wooden and lacklustre.

The programme was pre-recorded – it could not possibly have gone out live since people often stumbled over their words and had to have several goes at it. Most of the reviewers had never previously been near a television camera, so naturally they were nervous. They would arrive in Wells Street on Thursday afternoons and sit in a small room adjoining the studio, chatting to Fiona and me, until the technicians were ready. It was a bit like a dentist's waiting room. Once in the studio, they would be seated in a black leather chair, reminiscent of *Mastermind*. I would perch nearby, smiling encouragingly. When a green light came on, it was time to start reading from the autocue. Most people assume that feeling nervous speeds one up; but, as I soon realised, the opposite is almost invariably the case. I sometimes had to make conducting motions with my arms, like a kind of Toscanini of speech, to incite the speakers to speak more quickly.

But most of them needed no prompting; and some read with theatrical zest and 'listenability'. The crime writer Ruth Rendell, for example, was a mesmerising presence on the screen: she read aloud in a spooky monotone. Another outstanding performer was the ballerina Moira Shearer, who was also an accomplished writer. She 'spoke' a very unflattering review of an autobiography by Michael Powell, the man who directed the film *The Red Shoes* in which she had played the starring role. One of our youngest contributors – he must have been about 22 at the time – was the now famous historian Niall Ferguson. 'Book Choice' was presumably his first appearance on television and he took to it with astonishing confidence and panache – a natural. Niall had been recommended by his Cambridge tutor, the historian Norman Stone, who was an equally lively performer.

Others whom we used more than once because they spoke so forcefully and persuasively were the literature professor John Carey and the novelist Joanna Trollope.

Barbara Amiel, who was then a columnist for *The Times* and not yet the wife of the newspaper proprietor Conrad Black, told us that she was horribly apprehensive about whether she could do it. As soon as the green light went on, however, she became a complete professional.

The technicians who worked on *Book Choice* were only interested in its visual aspects. They insisted, for example, that the contributors must not wear anything stripy because this might cause 'strobing' – flickering light. They sometimes even demanded another take because a millimetre of someone's tweed jacket looked a bit fuzzy. At the same time they seemed totally unconcerned about the aural quality of the programme, which was surely its main purpose. This obsession with clarity of vision at the expense of clarity of sound seems still to be a feature of a majority of today's television programmes, as well as of many films. As a result it is often quite difficult to hear what performers on screen are saying. Later, in my role as arts editor, I commissioned an article on this subject, but of course no one in the TV or film world took the slightest notice.

V

The *Daily Telegraph*

By 1990, *Book Choice* had run its course. The genre of the spoken review has never, as far as I'm aware, been tried again – not surprisingly, perhaps. Meanwhile, at the end of 1986, I had been offered a full-time job, that of arts editor of the *Daily Telegraph* (I took Thursday afternoons off in order to continue with *Book Choice*). A former colleague at the *Observer*, Trevor Grove, who was then the *Telegraph*'s deputy editor (and would later become editor of the *Sunday Telegraph*), and to whom I will always feel grateful, had recommended me for it.

Working for a daily paper is far more demanding than working for a Sunday. Apart from anything else, it's a six-day-a-week job. But I found it exhilarating, not least because of the *Telegraph*'s dynamic new editor, Max Hastings. Though he had never before been an editor of any kind, Max was entrusted by the *Telegraph*'s new proprietor, the Canadian press baron Conrad Black, with the task of resuscitating and rejuvenating this ailing newspaper. It was still the most widely read daily broadsheet in Britain, but feeble management and greedy print unions had brought it to the edge of bankruptcy.

Max set about this modernising mission with ferocious energy. So much so that Black made the often quoted remark that 'Max was good at drowning kittens.' He said this admiringly, but it nevertheless seems to me a rather unfair choice of metaphor. It's true that Max had few qualms about sacking incompetent, ineffectual members of the staff. But most of these were the opposite of kittens – they were old lags comfortably coasting along while contributing very little of journalistic value to the paper. Max had no choice but to make many redundancies. Not that I would have wanted to be the target of Max's dissatisfaction: once he'd made up his mind, it snapped shut.

When Max took over, the average age of the critics in the arts department was 72. I have nothing against elderly journalists – their views are usually more insightful and interesting than those of unworldly novices. Indeed, the 'fresh-eye' approach, the notion that youth is preferable to experience, more often than not seems daft to me. But when, in the week or so before taking up the job, I carefully scrutinised the *Telegraph*'s arts pages, I realised that many of the articles were hackneyed and appeared to be written on auto-pilot. I too would have the unpleasant task of drowning one or two kittens. The first of these was the art critic. The abysmal quality of a piece by him on the painter John Constable took me aback. It was shoddily written, uninformative and dull. He apparently took very little trouble, or pride, in his job – a very privileged job at that.

With Max's agreement, I straight away arranged to

see this man (who was not, as it happened, particularly old, around 60, though he had been in the job for many years) and told him that I was so sorry but it was my intention to appoint a new art critic. He stared at me in astonishment and then, leaning as far as he could towards me across the desk separating us, he boomed: 'May I ask why?' Naturally, I didn't tell him that his work was not, in my view, good enough; it is (or was) particularly humiliating for a man to be sacked by a much younger woman. So I just mumbled that I had decided to appoint someone of my own choosing. Meanwhile, he kept bellowing 'Why, why, why?' Clearly, he thought I was mad.

By a great stroke of good fortune, I found a new art critic on the very next day. The first person I interviewed for the position seemed to me, correctly as it turned out, the ideal candidate: Richard Dorment, a forthright American-born art enthusiast – he had previously been a museum curator – who lived in London. He is still doing the job 25 years later, and has become one of England's most distinguished and trenchant writers on art.

Meanwhile, Max was successfully restoring the *Telegraph*'s fortunes. He introduced numerous imaginative new features, not least the daily cartoon by Matt. But he was also changing the paper's political character. To the distress of many Conservatives, young as well as old, he dragged it leftwards, abandoning its reliably right-wing, Thatcherite position in favour of his own liberal-conservative convictions. Indeed, he 'rebranded' the paper in rather the same way as David Cameron, more than twenty years later, was to rebrand the Conservative Party. Whether this ideological repositioning was a necessary component of the modernisation process is open to question. Personally I don't think it was, but then I was myself a Thatcher supporter. (In any event the *Telegraph*'s political stance has shifted several times since Max's day.)

Max's politics, however, didn't in the slightest detract from my admiration for him or from my enjoyment in working for him. Even his extreme impatience seemed sympathetic to me, probably because I am very impatient myself. At the daily editorial conference, for example, when the heads of department were required to outline what would appear on their pages that day, Max became visibly bored and fidgety if anyone so much as included a superfluous detail or made a single inconsequential remark. To keep Max's attention, one had to talk in telegraphese. Conferences, in consequence, were wonderfully – record-breakingly – short.

At the same time, and perhaps contrary to the general view of him, Max was immensely generous to and appreciative of his staff. Whenever he thought that one of us had done something particularly well, or had worked especially hard, he would send a handwritten 'hero-gram', praising our efforts. These memos were always beautifully phrased. And he even gave us personalised presents. Every Christmas, not only did he invite all the heads of department to a dinner at his grand London club (Brooks's), we would also all receive, each year, a charming enamel trinket box. I own four of these, all inscribed, inside the lid, with the date and the words 'From MH to MG, Thanks.'

Such thoughtfulness is rare among employers, not just in offices but in domestic settings as well. Yet having one's work appreciated seems to me a basic human need; and it immeasurably enhances the quality of one's working life. Any boss who doesn't notice, or doesn't want to notice, the efforts his employees are making on his behalf will soon lose their loyalty – and cause them to work less hard.

Being an arts editor is in many ways quite different from being a literary editor. For one thing, there are fewer decisions to be made. Instead of having to determine how to mix and match an endless stream of books and reviewers, all you need to do is make sure that the critics for the various art forms are as good as can be. Once that's done, the things they write about each day – new films, plays, ballets, exhibitions, television programmes – more or less dictate themselves.

Another difference is that, in those days, an art editor's 'perks' were even more enviable than those of a book editor or a woman's editor. To my delight and astonishment, I was given two free tickets to every artistic event (including Royal Opera House performances and Glyndebourne productions) that I wished to attend. The purpose behind this largesse was, presumably, to gain as much coverage for the events as possible. But it also enabled me to keep up with what was going on in the arts world; and to assess the quality of the critics – which is much easier if one has attended performances oneself.

Arts pages require a great deal of sub-editing, partly because critics on daily papers have to write in a great hurry for the next day's edition. Without sub-editors newspapers would be unreadable. They are an unsung category of journalist – 'super-editors' would be a better name for them. People outside journalism, and indeed outside book publishing, rarely realise to what extent minor alterations by skilled editors can produce major improvements. Often, the writers themselves are unaware that their prose has been made much more intelligible by small, subtle changes and cuts. Conversely, of course, an insensitive editor can ruin a good piece of writing in no time at all.

When I first worked at the *Telegraph*, every article and review was sent to the 'subs table', round which these clever people sat, correcting and improving the grammar, syntax and prose style of journalists – and writing witty, punning headlines. But most subs are better at working on news or sports stories than on arts reviews. When, soon after I arrived, Max decided to expand the arts coverage, I persuaded him that I needed two or three culturally inclined sub-editors to work exclusively for the arts department. I also wanted to continue doing at least some of the subbing myself as I had enjoyed doing this in my previous jobs.

Luckily, I managed to find a group of outstandingly gifted journalists to work with me. They all went on to greater things: Liz Anderson became an admired arts editor of the *Spectator* magazine; Charles Spencer turned into the *Telegraph*'s brilliant theatre critic; Kate Chisholm has written two much-praised literary biographies, and Peter Reed has taken up music criticism. At the time, they were highly skilled sub-editors, as well as delightful colleagues. I used to look forward every morning to spending the day with them (despite the dreadful journey to Canary Wharf, where the *Telegraph* moved long before the construction of the Jubilee Line). It was like having a second family.

With more arts pages to fill, we often ran feature articles as well as reviews. One that I was especially proud to have commissioned dealt with contemporary opera production. Many of the stagings of the operas I had been going to – whether it was Puccini's *Tosca* or Beethoven's *Fidelio* – resembled each other to an extraordinary degree. Having been wrenched from their original contexts, these operas were set in a more or less identical modern era – part totalitarian regime, part Mafia underworld. They shared a whole array of recurring motifs: choruses dressed in stripy prison pyjamas; a man in dark glasses sitting in a wheelchair; piles of scaffolding all over the place; a girl swaying aimlessly on a swing; people carrying suitcases from one side of the stage to the other. It was rare to find an opera (or a play, for that matter) that didn't contain two or more of the above.

The directors of these productions presumably thought they were introducing audiences to innovative, 'cutting-edge' ideas; in fact, they were churning out clichés. Michael Kennedy, the *Telegraph*'s chief music critic, agreed (he had joined the paper when he was fifteen and had become a leading expert on English music and the author of many authoritative books including the *Concise Oxford Dictionary of Music*). He wrote a very entertaining article on the subject.

Emotional life

'Love', wrote Byron in *Don Juan*, 'is of man's life a thing apart, 'Tis woman's whole existence.' I used to think that this was, roughly speaking, one of nature's laws. But now that more and more women are becoming heads of global companies or cabinet ministers, it seems increasingly likely that nurture has played at least as large a part as nature in the emotional make-up of many women. Most girls, from a very early age, are still undoubtedly much more immersed in their personal relationships than are young boys. But girls are now imbued with more self-esteem ('empowered') and may therefore be less prone to falling in love, and less anxious about finding the right partner. It's a question that has always puzzled me. Do these top women, particularly the younger ones, have love lives? And if they do, can they at the same time give their single-minded attention to their hugely important jobs? Or perhaps they have already found rock-like, Denis Thatcheresque partners? Or maybe a new tough species of female is in the process of evolving? Or are these chief-executive women just the exceptions that prove the rule?

In my case, unfortunately, Byron's aphorism was all too accurate. For a large part of my life, at school, at university and in various offices, my main preoccupation has been the ups and downs of my romantic involvements. Any work I managed to do during those years was in the teeth, so to speak, of some kind of emotional turmoil. Perhaps the fact that I had no roots in this country exacerbated this weakness – the feeling that my existence somehow needed validating by a bond with a man.

Certainly, during the four years I spent on the arts pages, my private life was in continuous disarray. On one level, I would be busy, for example, cutting repetitive bits out of a theatre notice (or removing the word 'searingly', as in 'searingly haunting', from concert reviews), or choosing photographs to illustrate a ballet feature; on another level, I would be agonising about my current romantic involvement. Why hadn't he returned my call? Was that a slighting remark he had made when we parted? Wasn't he, anyway, a wholly unsuitable partner for me?

Most people, to a greater or lesser extent, function on several layers simultaneously – rather like multiplex cinemas where different programmes are showing at the same time. Someone might be dutifully performing a day job in one part of his or her mind, while all kinds of competing narratives – a dysfunctional family saga, a conspiracy thriller, a steamy melodrama – are playing in other parts. If these scenarios become too tense or suspenseful, it is bound to affect one's concentration at work. Fortunately, or perhaps unfortunately, my job was not all that exacting.

It was during this time, in 1988, that John and I got divorced. Our marriage had broken down much earlier, in the 1970s, but we had stayed together, partly for the sake of our children, but mainly because we had become such close friends and allies. We knew and trusted each other completely and we saw the world through the same eyes. We almost never disagreed, either about politics or about people. But mental and spiritual closeness is perhaps less important in a marriage than physical compatibility. After 23 years, during which both of us had other relationships, we felt that it was time to make, as it were, an honest non-married couple of us. But our friendship didn't change. We talked to each other almost every day, often several times a day, until his death in 2011.

John was the most insightful person I have ever known. His analysis of any situation, private or public, was always sharply illuminating. For over 40 years he supported me in every aspect of my life. And in so far as I didn't have much family in England, John more than made up for it. In this respect, as in so many others, I have been extraordinarily fortunate.

After the failure of my marriage to John, I had a number of lengthy and serious relationships. None of them, in the end, worked out. The first and most distressing – and distracting – lasted for over six years. John and I, though still married, were living in separate parts of the house; but we never had any secrets from each other. Indeed, John was immensely kind to me throughout this time.

The man with whom I was involved was married, and I very much wanted him to set up home with me. As far as I was concerned, the purity of our feelings was such that there was no other honourable outcome. How naive and foolish – and stereotyped – I was. As I look back on it now, this love affair conformed in every particular to the familiar old plot of countless novels and dramas: vain and flirtatious married man amuses himself by seducing susceptible young woman and prolongs the affair with vague promises of an exclusive commitment as soon as the time is right. Meanwhile, he has no intention whatever of breaking up his marriage, which is in fact strengthened by his feelings of guilt. As long as I was part of it, though, I regarded my situation as unique – and it made me extremely miserable. I have never been a betrayed wife, thank goodness, but it can't be much worse than being the deluded 'other woman'.

Our relationship had to be conducted in complete secrecy. We would meet about once a week during lunchtimes, or for a drink at an obscure pub; very rarely there would be time for a furtive walk in Regent's Park. Quite often the man in question would cancel one of our meetings at the last moment, leaving me acutely disappointed.

Why did I (and why do others in similar situations) stay in such a one-sided relationship for so long? One obvious answer is that clandestine lovers meet in extraordinary circumstances. Their feelings are not subject to the changes that ordinary couples experience after the initial romantic excitement has worn off. Reality does not intrude into their 'brief encounters' and they can continue to idealise each other for years on end. Another answer has to do with the pain of rejection. Freud would argue that marital triangles replicate the unhappiness of the Oedipal situation, in which the adored parent favours his spouse over his child.

The theory of the Oedipus complex has never seemed wholly plausible to me, but I do believe that the intense unhappiness I felt during my relationship with a married man opened a wound of which I was barely aware – the wound caused by having felt abandoned by my parents in childhood. This must be true of others in similar relationships. It is often difficult to distinguish between pain and love – or at any rate, one is likely to love someone more if they reawaken an old pain. Be that as it may, I did eventually extricate myself from this involvement. It is the only thing I have ever done that required will-power. I did it by forcibly wrenching my affections in the direction of another 'love-object'.

By the time I left the *Daily Telegraph* to become literary editor of the *Sunday*, I had long given up on the notion that I would meet anyone resembling Mr Right, or indeed that there was such a thing. But in 1991 I found myself, by a miracle, seated next to this very person at a dinner. It was, in fact, a Booker prize dinner, and he was there as one of the guests from the 'non-literary' world, invited by a director of the company that sponsored the event. Geoffrey was a widower; a few months previously he had stepped down as editor of the *Financial Times* and switched to academia, becoming a fellow of the London School of Economics. Our first conversation was conducted entirely at cross purposes: he had just come back from Silicon Valley in California (where he had interviewed the computer pioneer Steve Jobs, among others). Meanwhile, I, in my ignorance about business, thought he was talking about silicone – the substance used for breast implants. Geoffrey was charmingly tolerant about my mortifying gaffe. But mainly, we talked about novels – he had been an avid fiction reader in his youth.

A day or two later, I mentioned to my friend and *Sunday Telegraph* colleague Anthea Hall, whose husband worked at the *Financial Times*, that I had sat next to, and much liked, its former editor. Anthea, who knew Geoffrey, immediately adopted the mantle of matchmaker. He had, she told me, been revered by the entire staff of the *FT* and had endured years of tragic family circumstances. I must immediately, she insisted, phone him and suggest a meeting – it would hugely cheer him up; it was just what he needed; I would be doing a good deed.

I had never in my life asked someone for a first date, but I happened to have two tickets for a performance of *The Marriage of Figaro* for the following day. I found a secluded office phone (no normal people owned mobiles at that time) and got through to Geoffrey at the London School of Economics: Sorry to disturb him but would he by any chance like to go to the opera with me on the following day? There was a short pause. 'Thank you so much – but I've got to go to a seminar.' A seminar? I felt that the word should be intoned with the same kind of disbelief as Lady Bracknell expresses in *The Importance of Being Ernest*: 'A handbag?'

Anyone who would rather go to a seminar than accompany me to the opera clearly wasn't in the slightest interested in embarking on a friendship with me. How humiliating. I upbraided Anthea for her very bad advice. She stood firm: Geoffrey was the kind of man who would never break an appointment just for his own gratification; he had, she felt sure, been pleased to hear from me. She turned out to be right. The following day, I received a letter from him asking me to the theatre.

We were married in 1993 and have lived very happily ever since. True romance, it appears, does exist, even in one's later years, and even within marriage. For me, it has brought the kind of stability – and freedom from doubts and uncertainties – that had been missing in much of my earlier life.

George Weidenfeld (left), making the speech at the reception of my wedding to Geoffrey Owen

The *Sunday Telegraph*

By the 1990s, the whole business of editing had become

in some ways much easier, thanks to the advent of new technology. Gone were messy typescripts covered in illegible handwritten corrections. Articles now looked immaculate – typing errors, spelling mistakes and grammatical howlers were a thing of the past. However, this outward appearance did not necessarily reflect the inner content. The actual writing was just as uneven as it had always been. Possibly more so because of the low priority that schools had been giving to writing skills. Editors were now confronted with what John Gross had termed 'the fallacy of neatness': an article might look so tidy and well ordered that an editor would be lulled into assuming that its substance was equally coherent. It required very careful reading to detect the repetitions and inconsistencies – not to mention the boring bits – that might be camouflaged by the flawless presentation.

One or two of our older contributors had not got to grips with computers. The most notable was the brilliant historian Hugh Trevor Roper (Lord Dacre). He still wrote his book reviews by hand and sent them in by post. In his case, though, the elegance of their appearance perfectly mirrored the elegance of his thoughts: he wrote in an exquisitely legible script with not a correction in sight and every sentence followed logically and lucidly from the one before.

I worked under three outstanding editors during my fourteen years (1991-2005) at the *Sunday Telegraph*. Trevor Grove for the first year or so, Charles Moore till 1995 and Dominic Lawson for the last ten years. All of them cared about literature and supported extensive book coverage. People often think that there has been a gradual dumbing-down in both the quantity and quality of literary journalism. But in the 1960s and 70s, newspapers devoted much less space to books, or to arts for that matter, than in the 1990s and 2010s. As for quality, the most distinguished critic I have ever worked with is Noel Malcolm (then in his thirties), the world's greatest authority on Thomas Hobbes and an expert on a whole range of other topics. The fortnightly reviews he wrote for the *Sunday Telegraph* while I was its literary editor (and subsequently too), were gems of lucidity, erudition and wit. And there were many other regular contributors who, it seems to me, were at least as good as the earlier generation of writers: Jonathan Bate, Caroline Moore, John Preston, Niall Ferguson, Kathryn Hughes, Selina Hastings, John Adamson, Jane Shilling, Andrew Roberts, David Robson, among many others.

Also contrary to the general view, critics, by and large, are very uncritical. They nearly always tend to over-praise. I know this, not just because I had myself read some of the books they reviewed, but because the reviewers would often tell me that a book to which they had given a rave notice was in reality fair to middling. Their benevolence has several causes. One is simply that critics, like most people, don't want to be disliked or to be regarded as spoilsports. Another is caution: as authors themselves, they fear that if they give a negative review to a fellow author he or she may one day be in a position to pay them back in kind. In addition, it is much safer, and less arduous, to praise. No one will hold you to account for your laudatory adjectives – but you have to be very sure of your ground to find fault. This applies especially to long books, of which some reviewers may not have read every word.

One of the rare critics who always says what he thinks is the clever journalist David Sexton, who was my deputy during the first few years at the *Sunday Telegraph*. David, it seems, doesn't care what anyone thinks of him, and as a result his reviews are often refreshingly honest – and negative. When they are positive you know he really means it. Naturally this has made him unpopular in some quarters. But he has many admirers, myself very much included. David left to become literary editor of the *Evening Standard* in 1996.

For the next decade, my other colleague, Michael Prodger, and I edited the substantial book section more or less on our own. (Once or twice a week we were assisted with sub-editing by the witty architectural historian Aileen Reid. Aileen is a PhD, rare in the world of journalism, and was known in the office as Doccy, short for Doctor).

Unlike other editorial departments, we also did the lay-outs and chose the pictures – tasks usually performed by the paper's art desk – which meant that we had total control of everything that appeared on our six broadsheet pages. Michael had two skills not usually found in the same person – unerring judgement in literary matters and mastery of computer technology. We developed a very happy working relationship, enhanced by the fact that we were both particularly interested in the visual side of journalism.

The *Telegraph* had a superb picture library containing vast quantities of photographs of historic figures and events, some of which had never been published. (They were mostly taken by staff photographers, now an extinct species.) One of our most pleasurable activities was sifting through dozens of these images in order to find the most appropriate pictures to illustrate our pages. We also devised some, as we thought, amusing photo-montages. For example, to accompany a review of a book about Australia by Bill Bryson, we had his head coming out of a kangaroo pouch. And we transformed the author Alain de Botton into a Roman philosopher by draping a toga round his shoulders and placing him on a plinth. This kind of thing has, since then, become much more common.

Every year, in January or February, we would hold a *Sunday Telegraph* books party to which all our contributors and various other friends and literary figures were invited. These parties were very successful, mainly for one reason – we offered champagne, lots of it. How could we afford such largesse? We did it with money derived from the sale of unwanted review copies. Our shelves would very quickly be filled to overflowing with books that publishers had sent in but that, for one reason or another, had not been reviewed. We needed to make room for the new books that poured in day after day. So every two or three weeks a book dealer would arrive at our office bringing numerous large crates and take dozens of books away. For each book he paid us a third of the sale-price (he would then sell these brand-new copies to libraries).

In this way, we amassed hundreds, indeed thousands, of pounds a year. The money would be handed over to me in cash. I would stuff it into a large envelope and lock it in my desk, first giving the people who worked for me a small sum – about £30 each – to supplement their incomes. By the end of the year we had collected at least £3000, easily enough to finance a large champagne party. This procedure might be regarded as ethically questionable, if not as downright theft. The books certainly did not belong to me. But to whom did they belong? Most probably they belonged to the paper's proprietor, Conrad Black, whom we must have been defrauding year after year.

The same thing used to go on when I worked at the *Observer*. Terry Kilmartin would give me and his secretary some pocket money and keep the rest. What he did with it I have no idea – perhaps he spent it on contributors and colleagues in the nearby pubs. Nor do I know what happens at other papers.

We would always keep back the most interesting and desirable books (those we hadn't already taken home ourselves) to give away at an annual Christmas bonanza (one hardback, one paperback, per person) for the entire *Sunday Telegraph* staff. Afterwards, people would thank me profusely, as though I was giving away my own books.

Our pages carried many book-related features as well as reviews. For example, we published a series in which we asked eminent people to say which books had made

them cry; and another in which business people chose
the novels which they thought dealt best with the world
of business and finance. At the end of the 1990s, we
devoted a whole page to the question: which were the
most influential books of the twentieth century. Twelve
well-read luminaries, among them the Nobel prize-
winning chemist Aaron Klug, the composer Michael
Tippett, the superstar Barry Humphries and the novelists
Muriel Spark and Doris Lessing selected ten books each.

The results were not especially surprising – Marcel
Proust and T.S. Eliot were chosen by nearly all of them.
Henry James, James Joyce, W.B. Yeats, Franz Kafka,
Evelyn Waugh and Joseph Conrad also got several
mentions. Two marvellous books that I was personally
very pleased to see included – bleak though they are –
were *If this is a Man*, Primo Levi's description of the year
he spent in Auschwitz extermination camp, and *Hope
Against Hope*, an autobiographical account of Stalin's
Russia by Nadezhda Mandelstam.

I had, by this time, been made 'group' associate editor
of the *Telegraph* – a nominal rather than a real promotion – which meant that I could go to editorial meetings and contribute to discussions about the contents
and editorial line of the two *Telegraph* papers and the
Spectator magazine. I did occasionally go to such meetings, but no one took much notice of what I said.
Literary people are regarded by most journalists, rightly
or wrongly, as somewhat off-beam when it comes to
politics and current affairs. I remember suggesting, several
times, under various different editors, that the paper

should send an Arabic-speaking undercover reporter to mosques around the country to ascertain what was being preached. This was in the mid-1990s, long before 9/11 but after the Ayatollah Khomeini had issued his fatwa (in 1989) against Salman Rushdie. The editors all thought this a good idea, but they never acted on it – mainly, I suspect, out of apathy. Indeed, I was constantly surprised at that time by the general lack of urgency on this subject: the state-sponsored death sentence pronounced on a novelist for alleged blasphemy had seemed to me then, and still seems to me today, one of the most shocking and eye-opening political incidents of my life; it perfectly encapsulated the difference between militant Islam and Western civilisation.

VI

Teaching

I stayed at the *Sunday Telegraph* until the age of 67. I had
felt uneasy about remaining beyond 65, which was then
retirement age, and had gone to see the editor, Dominic
Lawson, once or twice to talk to him about whether I
was outstaying my welcome – was it time for a younger
person – preferably Michael Prodger – to take over? He
always urged me to stay. But in 2005, when the *Telegraph*
management decreed that big savings on the editorial
side of the paper had to be made, Dominic called me to
his office and very politely suggested that I might like to
take up one of the large voluntary redundancy packages
that were then being offered. I instantly agreed. It later
turned out that old age pensioners were not eligible for
voluntary redundancy. But I would of course have left
anyway.

In any case, I had by that time had my fill of literary
journalism and was longing to do other things. I had
tried to branch out into another area many years previously, while still at the *Observer*. It had been suggested
to me by an acquaintance who was a justice of the peace
that I should volunteer to become a part-time magistrate.

I would be ideal, she said – just the kind of person they were looking for and, according to her, I could easily combine it with my work at the *Observer*. The idea very much appealed to me. My parents had, after all, both been lawyers, and I had always been interested in notions of justice. So I did all the preliminary homework and applied, supported by recommendations from various legal friends.

In due course I was interviewed by a panel of three leading magistrates. I can't now remember the two men who sat on either side, but the chairperson (she was indeed more like a chair than a person) was an unforgettable battleaxe. She had a large, square, wooden face surrounded by tight grey curls; she wore a brown tweed suit and sensible brown brogues and she was overflowing with self-confidence and a sense of her own British superiority. I can't now remember what questions she asked me, but I recall her hard little eyes and her clipped, imperturbable tones. (She was, I subsequently discovered, the wife of the then governor of the Bank of England.) A few weeks later, I received a letter informing me that I had been turned down. I was very upset, particularly by the last sentence of the letter: it stipulated that anyone who had failed to be appointed as a magistrate could never try to join the judiciary again.

So this area was barred to me. Instead, I worked as a part-time teacher – nearly 50 years since I'd last tried it. 'The tragedy of old age is not that one is old, but that one is young,' said Oscar Wilde. Old people have always claimed that, though they may look different from the outside, inside they feel exactly as they did when they were 22. This is certainly true of me. But it doesn't apply to teaching. This time round, with the experience and confidence of age, I found working with students unexpectedly easy and enjoyable.

I started at a charity school (Real Action) which had been set up in a deprived area of London to teach English literacy. Its pupils were mainly children who had fallen behind at school – but also some adults. Most of them were immigrants of various nationalities. I was asked to take a class made up of six or seven adults who already spoke quite good English. For a while, different pupils came and went, among them Brazilians, Chileans and Poles.

The person I most clearly remember from this time was a young Iranian woman who stayed for several weeks. Her beautiful face had been disfigured by many scars. We became friendly and she told me that acid had been thrown at her by a rejected suitor. According to her, this is not uncommon in Iran. She had fled to England and had been overwhelmed by the kindness shown to her here, particularly in the hospitals where she had undergone countless operations on her face. All English people, she kept saying, were 'angles'. It took me some time to work out that what she meant was 'angels'.

After a few months the make-up of my class became fairly settled. It consisted of six Somalis and one Eritrean, all of them Sunni Muslims, all of them intelligent and well educated. They had been to universities in various Arab and African countries and they were eager to improve their knowledge of England as well as their English. We would read aloud from newspapers and have political discussions. One of our standing jokes concerned the leftist philosopher Noam Chomsky, idolised in university departments of politics around the world, and in my view totally misguided. But despite their admiration for Chomsky, my students were largely pro-Western and fiercely opposed to terrorism and to Islamic extremism. Another of our jokes was their pronunciation of the word 'terrorist': it sounded exactly like 'tourist'. I often made them repeat the sentence 'I am a tourist not a terrorist.'

One of the Somalis worked at the Finsbury Park Mosque, where he was in charge of restoring normality after it had been turned into a centre for radicalisation by the notorious 'preacher of hate', Abu Hamza. The Eritrean, Edris, was the most academically inclined. He was very anxious to find a university where he could study for a PhD on the causes of the war between Ethiopia and Eritrea (1998-2000). Unfortunately, his English was not good enough. He himself had been severely injured in this war: one of his legs had been blown off (he walked with a prosthetic leg), and he had lost the use of one eye. Edris was touchingly stoical about his situation.

My students were very devout. If one of their five daily times for prayer happened to fall during a lesson, they would move a few desks out of the way, prostrate themselves on the floor and perform their ritual prayers. This lasted for three or four minutes, during which time I would stand against a wall at the side of the classroom. A surreal experience. I often worried about the fact that they didn't know that I was Jewish – ought I to tell them, even though I was totally secular? Was it relevant? Had they, like so many Muslims, been brought up to hate Jews? When I eventually mentioned it, they turned out to be rather philo-Semitic. Anti-Semitism, they said, was not part of Somali culture. They even wondered whether Jews were cleverer and more cultured than other people (after all, Chomsky was Jewish!). No, I told them, that was not so – some were, some weren't.

Sometimes four or five of 'my Somalis' came for tea at my house, and after a while they started coming for regular lessons there; it was much more convenient both for me and for them. This continued for about a year, but the students, for various reasons, gradually dispersed. One of them, Abdi (there were two Abdis in the class, Abdirahman and Abdihakim), the one who had worked at the Finsbury Park Mosque, became a junior minister in the beleaguered Somali transitional government. He was exceptionally tall, handsome and humorous, and the father of three small children. Since he left (his family remained in London), he has emailed me once or twice, saying that the situation in Mogadishu was terrible. There have been many terrorist attacks on government officials, and I worry about Abdi's safety.

Back to Jerusalem II
It was at about this time that my most recent visit to Israel took place. It came about in a rather unexpected way. I found myself seated, at a conference, next to a

distinguished and charming Israeli journalist, Danny Rubinstein, a columnist for the left-leaning paper *Ha'aretz*. He was about the same age as me and had also been born in Jerusalem. But talking about our common background turned out to be a somewhat embarrassing experience for me. What school had I attended? he asked. Alas, I couldn't remember its name. What about the names of any teachers? Again, sorry, can't remember. OK, surely you can recall the names of some school friends. Well yes, I remember the name of one girl, who had been my best friend – Ruth. Ruth what? It was almost exactly 60 years ago, I protested; sorry, no, I can't remember. 'Well', he said, 'I regard this as a challenge. I am flying back to Jerusalem tomorrow and I will find your Ruth.' I gave him my email address, but I thought it highly unlikely that he would succeed, or even try. There must be hundreds of Ruths in Jerusalem.

He was as good as his word. A few days after our meeting he emailed to say that he had found my Ruth. It had taken only a few phone calls. My Ruth was Ruth Meyuchas (the surname rang an immediate bell), a good friend of his. She remembered me well.

A day or two later, I got a phone call from Ruty (as she was known) who sounded so friendly and jolly that I was instantly drawn to her. We decided to email each other our life stories, starting from the time we had last seen each other, at the age of eight or nine.

So began a very candid and absorbing correspondence, which proceeded by chronological instalments. It lasted for about three months. Every day we would eagerly await the arrival of a new episode and, like Victorian novelists, we sometimes deliberately ended on a cliff-hanger, so as to make our narratives more exciting. Ruty's English was good – she had spent three years in England – but she often wrote to say that she wished she could express herself with more subtlety and nuance. Our stories could hardly have been more different: Ruty's life resembled an action thriller while mine was more akin to a romantic novelette.

Ruty had deep roots in Israel. Her father was a Sephardic Jew whose family had come to Palestine in the nineteenth century; her mother's family had also arrived several generations ago, from Russia. Ruty had been brought up with a strong sense of duty to the nation, as a pioneer and a volunteer. After doing her military service she had, among other things, co-founded a kibbutz, worked in various psychiatric clinics and addiction centres and helped integrate immigrants from Morocco, India, Iraq and elsewhere. Later, she had founded Israel's first organisation to help dyslexic students and had been involved in establishing a nationwide network of nursery schools.

In her forties, she was invited – 'out of the blue moon' as she put it – to work in the Knesset (the Israeli parliament) as a civil servant, where she eventually rose to become head of the Foreign Relations Department. Along the way, Ruty had brought up three sons, and she had experienced the hardships and terrors of war.

By contrast, my life, with its succession of desk jobs and string of romantic entanglements, seemed hopelessly commonplace. But, as Ruty very kindly put it when I half-jokingly pointed out that her life had been much more 'real' than mine: 'You didn't have outside wars, but many wars inside yourself.'

When our narratives finally reached the present day, Ruty invited me to a party she was giving for her women friends. Would I like to come, and spend the weekend in Jerusalem? Yes, indeed I would.

Meeting someone in person for the first time (or for the first time after 60 years), when you have been in continuous, close communication for some months, is a disconcerting experience. We had exchanged jokey descriptions of our current grandmotherly appearance, but inevitably Ruty was subtly different from the way I had imagined her. She had a round, attractive face and a warm smile, but what mainly surprised me was that I had expected an immediate sense of intimacy – and this was absent. Our conversation on the drive to Jerusalem was amicable, but distant.

It is not possible, I realised when I thought about it later, to build intimacy just through a correspondence, however revealing and confessional it may have been. Intimacy needs much more time and much more physical togetherness than Ruty and I had shared.

Her party was attended by about 40 women – civil servants, doctors, professors of archaeology, lawyers, art-historians, journalists – all close friends of Ruty's. I have never before, or since, been to a gathering where there was such a strong feeling of mutual trust, openness and equality. None of the elements that so often impair the enjoyment of social gatherings in England – cliquishness, social insecurity, insincerity, and so on – were present. Ruty's friends had spent their lives working for a cause – to make Israel a viable and civilised state – and they had lived through wars and dangerous times together. I was hugely impressed and attracted by them but at the same time I felt very English, and very much an outsider. The party continued late into the afternoon, with some dancing and singing. I attempted, very self-consciously, to join in.

Ruty took immense trouble to make my weekend as action-packed as possible. She introduced me to all kinds of interesting and friendly people (some of them old classmates). The question that nearly all of them asked me was: 'Why did you leave Israel?' My reply, that it had been my parents' decision, not mine, seemed not quite to satisfy them. Perhaps I was imagining this – there was certainly nothing overtly reproachful in anyone's reaction – but I felt an unasked question hovering in the air: why hadn't I come back when I was old enough to make my own decisions?

How would I have replied? The truth is that it never occurred to me to return to Israel. I greatly admired the country's achievements – its democratic way of life, its outstanding universities, its cultural attainments, its contributions to medicine and so on – but I had no family or friends there and I no longer spoke Hebrew. I had been brought up, for better or worse, without any sense of religious or ethnic identity, but I had, meanwhile, acquired a strong sense of English cultural identity. So I had no incentive to go back. Moreover, the notion that people should be judged as individuals, not as members of a group (or for that matter gender), had been instilled in me from an early age.

Of course, Jews share a common history, a history of appalling persecution. My parents, my grandparents and I are part of it. I remember having an argument about anti-Semitism with my father when I was a teenager. He had said that, however horrified and remorseful people felt about the Holocaust, however much they claimed that such a thing could never happen again, prejudice against Jews would reappear in about 50 years' time. I poured scorn on this view, reproving my father for being defeatist and out of touch. Now I know better. The virus of anti-Semitism is passed on from generation to generation. It is almost impossible to shake off prejudices that have been embedded in childhood, by parents or teachers or preachers. Besides, very few people would easily give up the idea that there is someone, or some group, that they can despise and blame for their own misfortunes and shortcomings.

In some parts of the world anti-Semitism has become even more widespread than my father predicted. So the existence of a country where Jews will always be welcome is as important now as it was when my parents went to Palestine in 1933. There is plenty of anti-Jewish feeling in England too; but I firmly believe that it is a country where racism of any kind will never be allowed to flourish. 'The English people are not good haters...' George Orwell wrote in 1947, '...to twentieth-century political theories they oppose, not another of their own, but a moral quality which must be vaguely described as decency.' This seems to me still to hold true in the 21st century. It is one of the reasons that makes me proud to be English, or almost English.

Interviews

published in the Observer *1979-85*

PHILIP LARKIN
1979

I had not met Philip Larkin before we did our interview, but from talking to various of his friends, from studying his photograph and of course from reading his poems and novels, I had formed a strong impression of the kind of person he would be: lugubrious, depressed, polite, shy, tense, unforthcoming, physically unprepossessing, charming. As soon as I met him, I realised that more than half those adjectives didn't fit – at least not on this particular day. He greeted me, when I entered his spacious office at the University of Hull where he had been chief librarian for 25 years, in a friendly, positively jovial manner. There wasn't a trace of gloom about him. If he had ever been shy (which surely he must have been), he had clearly cured himself of this disability. His appearance, too, confounded my expectations: he was taller than I imagined and had a much more imposing physical presence. Throughout our interview he was relaxed and forthcoming, jokey and even flirtatious. Definitely charming.

Only once, during the two or three hours I spent with him, did the Larkin of the darker poems show through. Before we started the interview, while I was setting up my tape recorder, he said, almost in passing, and in a matter-of-fact tone of voice, that were it not for his job as librarian, he would long ago have killed himself.

MIRIAM GROSS: Like most of your readers, I suppose, I've been struck by how much your poems are about unhappiness, loss, a sense of missing out. Do you think

this is really a fair impression of the way you see life?
PHILIP LARKIN: Actually, I like to think of myself as quite funny, and I hope this comes through in my writing. But it's unhappiness that provokes a poem. Being happy doesn't provoke a poem. As Montherlant says somewhere: happiness writes white. It's very difficult to write about being happy. Very easy to write about being miserable. And I think writing about unhappiness is probably the source of my popularity, if I have any – after all most people are unhappy, don't you think?

Do you think people go around feeling they haven't got out of life what life has to offer?
I should think quite a lot of people do. Whether Lew Grade does, or Harold Wilson, I don't know. But that's what I see. Deprivation is for me what daffodils were for Wordsworth.

Tell me a bit about your childhood. Was it really as 'unspent' as you suggest in one of your poems?
Oh, I've completely forgotten it. My father was a local government official and we lived in quite respectable houses and had a succession of maids and that sort of thing, as one did before the war. It was all very normal: I had friends whom I played football and cricket with and Hornby trains and so forth.

It was perhaps not a very sophisticated childhood, although the house was full of books. My father was keen on Germany for some reason: he'd gone there to study their office methods and fallen in love with the place. And he took us there twice; I think this sowed the seed of my hatred of abroad – not being able to talk to anyone, or read anything.

As for school, I was an unsuccessful schoolboy. You must remember that I was very short-sighted and nobody realised it, and also that I stammered, so that really classes were just me sitting with bated breath dreading lest I should be called

on to say something. Eventually most of the masters understood and I wasn't bothered – just left alone. I cheered up a
bit in the sixth form where the classes were smaller and most
things were just across a table.

Did you feel as a child you were somehow an outsider?
Well, I didn't much like other children. Until I grew up I
thought I hated everybody, but when I grew up I realised
it was just children I didn't like. Once you started meeting
grown-ups life was much pleasanter. Children are very
horrible, aren't they? Selfish, noisy, cruel, vulgar little brutes.
And if you've ever stammered, that's enough to make you
feel an outsider – though I think shyness is contagious, you
know. I remember when I was quite young telling my father
I was shy, and he said very crushingly, 'You don't know what
shyness is,' implying that he'd been much more shy. Probably
both my parents were rather shy people – of each other, of
their children.

I was wondering whether in the new *Oxford Dictionary of
Quotations* I was going to be lumbered with 'They fuck you
up, your mum and dad'. I had it on good authority that
this is what they'd been told is my best-known line, and I
wouldn't want it thought that I didn't like my parents. I did
like them. But at the same time they were rather awkward
people and not very good at being happy. And these things
rub off.

Anyway, they didn't put that line in. Chicken, I suppose.
For the most part the things they did put in I shouldn't have
thought were on everybody's lips. If someone asked me what
lines I am known for it would be the one about mum and
dad or 'Books are a load of crap' – sentiments to which every
bosom returns an echo, as Dr Johnson said – or, rising a
little in the spiritual scale, 'What will survive of us is love',
or 'Nothing, like something, happens anywhere'. They did
include that one, actually.

Can you remember when exactly you started writing?

The same age that everybody starts – at puberty, which admittedly was a little later in my day than I understand it is now. Fifteen, sixteen. I remember the first poem I ever wrote was set for homework. We had to write one, about anything. We were all absolutely baffled and consternation reigned. The poem I turned in was terrible.

But did you have an inkling when you wrote it that you might write other poems?

No. You must realize I didn't want to write poems at all, I wanted to write novels. I started writing *Jill* immediately I left Oxford in 1943. It was published by the Fortune Press in 1946, which was already two years after it was finished, and by that time I had written my second novel, *A Girl in Winter*. I distinctly remember racing away at the final revision just about VE day – a very Prousty way of disregarding external distractions. It was published by Faber in the great freeze-up of 1946-7, in February – very appropriate in view of the title, almost like a cosmic publicity campaign. And I thought this was it, I'm made. But I could never write a third novel, though I must have spent about five years trying to. I felt a bit cheated. I'd had visions of myself writing 500 words a day for six months, shoving the result off to the printer and going to live on the Cote d'Azur, uninterrupted except for the correction of proofs. It didn't happen like that – very frustrating.

I still think novels are much more interesting than poems – a novel is so spreading, it can be so fascinating and so difficult. I think they were just too hard for me. I've said somewhere that novels are about other people and poems are about yourself. I think that was the trouble, really. I didn't know enough about other people, I didn't like them enough.

Tell me about your Oxford days.

Oxford terrified me. Public-school boys terrified me. The
dons terrified me. So did the scouts. And there was the
stammer: I still stammered quite badly up to the age of
maybe 30. I mean stammered to the point of handing over
little slips of paper at the railway station saying third-class
return to Birmingham instead of actually trying to get it
out. Still, I soon had several circles of friends at Oxford. The
college circle, the jazz circle, possibly the literary circle. And
I don't want to give the impression that there was a great
divide between public-school boys and grammar-school
boys. You see nobody had anything in those days, in the war.
Everybody wore the same utility clothes. There was one kind
of jacket, one kind of trousers; no cars; one bottle of wine
a term. The distinctions between different classes of undergraduates were really pruned back.

And what do you think about Oxford now?

Well, I don't know much about it. Of course the big change
since my day is the invasion of women in men's colleges.

**'Invasion' seems rather a loaded word. Does that mean
you don't approve of it?**

I don't know. I suppose I'm a little suspicious of it: one's
always suspicious of change. One wonders what the effect
will be on what is, after all, the ostensible purpose of universities – learning, teaching, research and so on. On the other
hand I see nothing against it in theory, and I'm a little
envious, too: it would have been nice to have been part of
the experiment. But I'd like to know what the result is in ten
years' time: whether they will have settled down into a kind
of unisex community or whether it will boil up into shoot-
ings and tears and failed exams and nervous breakdowns.
Probably something cheerful and non-academic, like an
American college musical.

You mentioned jazz. How did your interest in it start?

It started as soon as I heard anything with four beats to the bar, which was, in my early days, dance music. Jack Payne, Billy Cotton, Harry Roy. I listened to bands like that for an awfully long time without realising that there was such a thing as American jazz.

I must have learned dozens of dance lyrics simply by listening to dance music. I suppose they were a kind of folk poetry. Some of them were pretty awful, but I often wonder whether my assumption that a poem is something that rhymes and scans didn't come from listening to them – and some of them were quite sophisticated. 'The Venus de Milo was noted for her charms / But strictly between us, you're cuter than Venus/And what's more you've got arms' – I can't imagine Mick Jagger singing that; you know, it was witty and technically clever.

I always think of Ray Noble's 'Tiger Rag' as my first jazz record: not really very jazzy but it was a jazz number; and the second one I bought was the Washboard Rhythm Kings' 'I'm gonna play down by the Ohio', which I've still got. And the third was Louis Armstrong's 'Ain't Misbehavin'. Of course once I'd got that the way was clear.

Did you dance as well as listen to jazz?

Dance, you mean dance? Dancing was very much more formal in those days. Not a jazz thing. For one thing you had to do it with somebody else; you couldn't dance alone. That presented problems for a start if you hadn't got somebody else. Secondly, it was very difficult. I never learned to dance in a conventional sense: those books you learned from, with black feet and white feet and dotted lines, baffled me completely.

What about your being a librarian? What made you become one?

I came on to the labour market in the middle of the First –
Christ, I mean the Second World War. Owing to bad eyesight
I wasn't called up for military service, and the number of jobs
available were few and far between.

I tried twice to get into the Civil Service but the Civil
Service didn't want me, and I was sitting at home quietly
writing *Jill* when the Ministry of Labour wrote to me asking,
very courteously, what I was doing exactly. This scared
me and I picked up the *Birmingham Post* and saw that an
urban district council in Shropshire wanted a Librarian, so
I applied and got it. But looking back it was an inspired
choice. Librarianship suits me – I love the feel of libraries
– and it has just the right blend of academic interest and
administration that seems to match my particular talents,
such as they are. And I've always thought that a regular job
was no bad thing for a poet. Indeed, Dylan Thomas himself
– not that he was noted for regular jobs – said this; you can't
write more than two hours a day, and after that, what do you
do? Probably get into trouble.

I'm fond of saying [broad Yorkshire] I started at the bottom.
I had to do everything in that Shropshire library: I drew the
line at cleaning the floor, but I stoked the boiler and kept
it going through the day, served the children, put up the
papers and so on. And in the evenings I took a correspondence course to get my professional qualifications. I'm still a
member of the Library Association: I bought its tie the other
day.

In any case, I could never have made a living from writing.
If I'd tried in the 40s and 50s I'd have been a heap of
whitened bones long ago. Nowadays you can live by being a
poet. A lot of people do it: it means a blend of giving readings and lecturing and spending a year at a university as
poet in residence or something. But I couldn't bear that: it
would embarrass me very much. I don't want to go around
pretending to be me.

Can you tell me something about the way you write a poem?

It varies a great deal. A poem can come quickly. You just write it all out and then the next evening you alter a word or two and it's done. Another time it will take longer, perhaps months. What is always true is that the idea for a poem and a bit of it, a snatch or a line – it needn't be the opening line – come simultaneously. In my experience one never sits down and says I will now write a poem about this or that, in the abstract.

Do you feel terribly pleased when you've written one?

Yes, as if I've laid an egg, and even more pleased when I see it published. Because I do think that's a part of it: you want it to be seen and read, you're trying to preserve something. Not for yourself, but for the people who haven't seen it or heard it or experienced it.

What about your politics? For example, you talk in one poem about troops being brought home from various parts of the world...

Well, that's really history rather than politics. That poem has been quoted in several books as a kind of symbol of the British withdrawal from a world role. I don't mind troops being brought home if we'd decided this was the best thing all round, but to bring them home simply because we couldn't afford to keep them there seemed a dreadful humiliation. I've always been right-wing. It's difficult to say why, but not being a political thinker, I suppose I identify the Right with certain virtues and the Left with certain vices. All very unfair, no doubt.

Which virtues and vices?

Well, thrift, hard work, reverence, desire to preserve – those are the virtues, in case you wondered: and on the other hand idleness, greed and treason.

What do you think about Mrs Thatcher?
Oh, I adore Mrs Thatcher. At last politics makes sense to me, which it hasn't done since Stafford Cripps (I was very fond of him too). Recognising that if you haven't got the money for something you can't have it, this is a concept that's vanished for many years. I'm delighted to see it surfacing again. But I'm afraid I don't think she will succeed in changing people's attitudes. I think it's all gone too far. What will happen to this country I can't imagine.

Tell me what you like reading.
I read everything except philosophy, theology, economics, sociology, science, or anything to do with the wonders of nature, anything to do with technology – have I said politics? I'm trying to think of all the Dewey decimal classes. In point of fact I virtually read only novels, or something pretty undemanding in the non-fiction line, which might be a biography. I read almost no poetry. I always thought the reading habits of Dylan Thomas matched mine – he never read anything hard.

I tend to go back to novelists, like Dick Francis, for instance; I've just been through his early novels again, which I think are outstandingly good for what they are. And Barbara Pym, of course, whom I've written about. Dickens, Trollope – sometimes you go back to them for about three novels running. And detective stories: Michael Innes – I don't know why there has never been a serious study of him: he's a beautifully sophisticated writer, very funny and, now and then, very moving. Anthony Powell, Rex Stout, Kingsley Amis, Peter de Vries.

And what about poetry?
I read Betjeman, Kingsley again, Gavin Ewart (who I think

is extraordinarily funny). Among the illustrious dead, Hardy and Christina Rossetti. Shakespeare, of course. Poetry can creep up on you unawares. Wordsworth was nearly the price of me once. I was driving down the M1 on a Saturday morning: they had this poetry slot on the radio, 'Time for Verse'; it was a lovely summer morning, and someone suddenly started reading the Immortality ode, and I couldn't see for tears. And when you're driving down the middle lane at 70 miles an hour... I don't suppose I'd read that poem for twenty years, and it's amazing how effective it was when one was totally unprepared for it.

A bibliography of your work has just been published. What do you feel about being bibliographed?
On the whole, very flattered, as long as no one thinks I thought all these things worth exhuming. Barry Bloomfield is a first-class bibliographer, and it's surprising what he dug out.

Do you get much out of reading criticism of your work?
Well, there isn't an awful lot of it. I may flatter myself, but I think in one sense I'm like Evelyn Waugh or John Betjeman, in that there's not much to say about my work. When you've read a poem, that's it; it's all quite clear what it means.

What about the themes that run through your poetry – not getting married, for instance?
Is that one of my themes? I don't think it is anything very personal. I find the idea of always being in company rather oppressive; I see life more as an affair of solitude diversified by company than an affair of company diversified by solitude.

I don't want to sound falsely naive, but I often wonder why people get married. I think perhaps they dislike being alone more than I do. Anyone who knows me will tell you that I'm not fond of company. I'm very fond of people, but it's difficult to get people without company. And I think living with someone and being in love is a very difficult business anyway because almost by definition it means putting yourself at the disposal of someone else, ranking them higher than yourself. I wrote a little poem about this which was never collected so perhaps you never saw it. Do you know it? 'The difficult part of love/Is being selfish enough/Is having the blind persistence /To upset someone's existence/Just for your sake – / What cheek it must take.' End of first verse. 'Then take the unselfish side – /Who can be satisfied/Putting someone else first,/So that you come off worst?/My life is for me:/As well deny gravity.' There is a third verse, but that's the gist of it. I think love collides very sharply with selfishness, and they're both pretty powerful things.

Do you like living in Hull?
I don't really notice where I live; as long as a few simple wants are satisfied – peace, quiet, warmth – I don't mind where I am. As for Hull, I like it because it's so far away from everywhere else. On the way to nowhere, as somebody put it. It's in the middle of this lonely country, and beyond the lonely country there's only the sea. I like that.

  I love all the Americans getting onto the train at King's Cross and thinking they're going to come and bother me, and then looking at the connections and deciding they'll go to Newcastle and bother Basil Bunting instead. Makes it harder for people to get at you. I think it's very sensible not to let people know what you're like. And Hull is an unpretentious place. There's not so much crap around as there would be in London, at least as I imagine it, or in some other university cities.

So you don't ever feel the need to be at the centre of things? You don't want to see the latest play, for instance?

Oh no, I very much feel the need to be on the periphery of things. I suppose when one was young one liked to be up to date. But I very soon got tired of the theatre. I count it as one of the great moments of my life when I first realised one could actually walk out of a theatre. I don't mean offensively – but go to the bar at the interval and not come back. I did it first at Oxford: I was watching *Playboy of the Western World* and when the bell rang at the interval I asked myself: 'Am I enjoying myself? No, I've never watched such stupid balls.' So I just had another drink and walked out into the evening sunshine.

What about travel? Wouldn't you like to visit, say, China?
I wouldn't mind seeing China if I could come back the same day. I hate being abroad. Generally speaking, the further one gets from home the greater the misery. I'm not proud of this, but I'm singularly incurious about other places. I think travelling is very much a novelist's thing.

A novelist needs new scenes, new people, new themes. The Graham Greenes, the Somerset Maughams: travelling is necessary for them. I don't think it is for poets. The poet is really engaged in recreating the familiar; he's not committed to introducing the unfamiliar.

Do you think much about growing older? Is it something that worries you?
Yes, dreadfully. If you assume you're going to live to be 70, seven decades, and think of each decade as a day of the week, starting with Sunday, then I'm on Friday afternoon now. Rather a shock, isn't it? If you ask why does it bother me, I can only say I dread endless extinction.

Do you feel you could have had a much happier life?
Not without being someone else. I think it is very much

easier to imagine happiness than to experience it. Which is a pity because what you imagine makes you dissatisfied with what you experience, and may even lead you to neglect it. 'Life, and the world, and mine own self, are changed/For a dream's sake,' to quote Christina Rossetti. Though I think that a point does come in life when you realize that there's a limit to what you can get from other people and there's a limit to what your own personality is in itself. That's really the story of *A Girl in Winter*.

Do you feel worried about people not reading poetry in the future?

No, I'm much more worried about poetry becoming official and subsidised. I think we got much better poetry when it was all regarded as sinful or subversive, and you had to hide it under the cushion when somebody came in. What I don't like about subsidies and official support is that they destroy the essential nexus between the writer and the reader. If the writer is being paid to write and the reader is being paid to read, the element of compulsive contact vanishes.

I should hate anybody to read my work because he's been told to and told what to think about it. I really want to hit them; I want readers to feel: yes, I've never thought of it that way, but that's how it is.

FRANCIS BACON
1980

Francis Bacon didn't like giving interviews and it was only to oblige Sonia Orwell, an old friend of his who had asked him on my behalf, that he agreed to do one with me. Nevertheless, he was extraordinarily courteous throughout our time together.

In the first place, he insisted that I join him and a friend – a good-looking, polite young man – for lunch at a smart Chelsea restaurant. When we sat down, he straight away ordered a bottle of champagne. As far as I was aware at that time, champagne was only opened for celebrations, so I was momentarily taken aback. But it soon became apparent that this was his habitual lunchtime drink. His conversation, too, surprised me. I had naively expected him to be a slightly thuggish character who would exude an air of suppressed violence. Not a bit of it. Throughout lunch he talked passionately and knowledgeably about literature, particularly about Proust, whose work he knew in daunting detail.

After lunch he took me to his studio, and this was even more astounding. It looked like a caricature of an artist's studio. Every inch of every wall from floor to ceiling was splattered with blobs of thick, multi-coloured paint. I felt as though I had walked into a three-dimensional painting by Jackson Pollock. This seemed particularly odd when contrasted with the sleek, smooth, un-Jackson-Pollocky brush-strokes of Bacon's own work. There was, however, one Baconian touch: a bare light bulb dangled at the end of a long flex from the centre of the ceiling.

MIRIAM GROSS: When did you first have any idea or intimation that you might become a painter?

FRANCIS BACON: I never really thought about it. I didn't start painting till I was about 30: I was in Paris and I saw an exhibition of Picasso's and I thought, well, why shouldn't I try and paint? And that's really how it started.

You see, I came from a family – my father was a trainer of racehorses – where no one was the slightest bit interested in any of the arts. And in Ireland, where I mostly grew up, we never really went to school. I don't know whether that's a good thing or a bad thing. My father didn't believe in schooling, my mother absolutely adored entertaining – giving parties and that kind of thing – and they were so busy enjoying their social life that they didn't want to spend much money on their children.

And what kind of life did you lead as a young man?
I left home when I was sixteen or so, and I didn't work at anything very much. I had friends who were very kind to me; and I can't say that when I was young I was at all honest. I used to steal money from my father whenever I could, and I was always taking rooms in London and then disappearing – not paying the rent, not being able to pay it. What's called morality has grown on me with age. But in those days I managed to get by on petty theft and on living off people.

I did have one or two jobs at that period. I worked as a servant, for example, for a solicitor in Mecklenburgh Square: I had to be there early in the morning to get his breakfast, then I was supposed to 'do' the place and come back in the evening to cook the dinner. When I gave in my notice, as they say, I always remember him saying, 'I don't know why he's bothering to go because he never does anything.' I also worked in a wholesale shop for women's clothes in Poland Street, in Soho. I knew nothing about the business; they more or less employed me just to answer the telephone.

I never thought about painting at all during that time. I did try to do some furniture designing but it was entirely influenced by the German and French things being done then. There was nothing at all original about it.

Do you think that not going to art school or having any kind of formal training has helped you or hindered you as a painter?
Well, I don't think that in a time like ours, when there's no tradition at all, there's anything you can possibly teach. I remember I once stood in for a friend, Johnnie Minton, who asked me if I'd take over his job for two or three months at

the Royal College of Art – which I did. But I couldn't teach anything at all. All I could do was go there, for two days a week, and if the students wanted someone to talk to, I was there.

You don't think that being taught draughtsmanship, life drawing or that sort of thing, helps?
I don't think it does. One sees the people who have been taught, who are painting nowadays. What are they doing? After all, they never make anything new, they just go back to a kind of academic drawing which would have been much better done by artists in the past.

The first of your paintings which really caught people's attention was the *Figures at the Base of a Crucifixion* which is in the Tate, and you've painted other studies of crucifixion as well. As far as I know you're not religious, and I wonder why you were so strongly drawn to this subject.
It was not through belief and it was not through disbelief that I did them. It was because there was no image that interested me as much at the time, and I was interested in the way it had been used in the past. After all, some of the greatest paintings of the West have been inspired by that theme. I was very influenced, for instance, by photographs I'd seen of the Grünewald Crucifixion, and also the Cimabue one, in Florence.

But weren't you also drawn to it as a symbol of suffering and cruelty?
Well, I don't know… People always seem to think that in my paintings I'm trying to put across a feeling of suffering and the ferocity of life, but I don't think of it at all in that way myself. You see, just the very fact of being born is a very ferocious thing, just existence itself as one goes between

birth and death. It's not that I want to emphasise that side of things – but I suppose that if you're trying to work as near to your nervous system as you can, that's what automatically comes out. Unless you put a veil between yourself and life, it is just filled, really, with suffering and despair.

To what extent do you think an artist's experience of life, of suffering, goes into his painting? Do you yourself paint under the influence of emotions that are going on in your life?

No. I don't really know what I'm doing: I just put down the images and I hope that I will be able to excite myself.

A lot of your paintings do undoubtedly convey a sense of despair and often shock – one feels that the human figures in them are in the process of turning into a different kind of creature.

For me the distortions in my work are not there for the sake of distortion, but to bring back, as it were, the reality of the image – to bring it back as strongly as I can onto my own nervous system. I'm not setting out to give any feeling of horror; I'm just attempting to record my own sensibility, my own sensations – which seems to me the only thing one can do at a time when there's no longer any tradition in art.

Have you ever been tempted to do any purely abstract painting?

Well, I did design a few rugs and things which were totally abstract, but I don't think I've ever done an abstract painting. I feel that on the whole abstract art is a form of decoration. Possibly there could be tremendous bursts of colour, but you've had that at its best with people like Turner and Monet – and there the colour was used for a reason. If it isn't, it automatically becomes just decorative.

In your marvellous book of conversations with David Sylvester you say that you've always been interested in the mouth as an image. I think you say that you would have liked to do a Monet-like version of a mouth.

If you think of all those wonderful paintings by Monet, the Monet of the Nympheas especially – well, the mouth, if one looks at it, the tongue and the lips and the teeth and everything, has got all those colours in it. Also, when I was young, I think it was in a second-hand bookshop in Paris, I found a book on diseases of the mouth with very beautiful illustrations, and they fascinated me. I'm sure that psychoanalysts and people like that would say that there are much deeper reasons, but I don't know.

And do you paint the images of meat that one finds in your paintings for the same kind of reason?

Yes, it's to do with colour. You've only got to go into a butcher's shop – it's nothing to do with mortality, as people often think, it's to do with the great beauty of the colour of meat.

A lot of your paintings are triptychs and a lot of your figures seem to be in motion. Do you think you've been influenced in all this by the cinema?

Yes, I do. I think that if I'd been born later, rather than trying to paint, I'd have attempted to make films. I think it's a medium which hasn't been really explored yet.

I know that one image which made an enormous impact on you was the famous shot of the screaming nurse in *The Battleship Potemkin*. That surely is another moment of extreme anguish.

Yes, but I don't think it's the anguish in it that appealed to me: it was the beauty of that shot, the mouth, and I was excited by the idea of it being done in colour, the colour of the lips and the flesh and tongue.

What about your series of popes – some of them are screaming, too.

I don't think they were at all successful: I was hypnotised by two things at that time: Eisenstein's screaming nurse, and Velazquez's portrait of Pope Innocent X, and I thought I would try to catch something of the beauty of the Velazquez and the beauty of the scream in the same image. I think I must have been terribly immature; if I'd thought more about it I would never have done those paintings. You see, they look as though one was searching for a form of sensationalism, and perhaps one was in one's immaturity. I can't remember back, but I look at them now really with disgust.

Haven't you also done some paintings inspired by Van Gogh?

Yes, I was having an exhibition at the Hanover Gallery and I absolutely couldn't paint anything, and about two weeks before the exhibition was due to open I thought, oh well, I can't do anything now, I'll just do some things influenced by Van Gogh. I'm afraid only one of them worked at all, a figure walking down a slope.

For me, Van Gogh is one of the very greatest painters who have ever lived; what I admire is his ability to put across a tremendously complex sensation in such a simple way. People often assume he was a simple man, but if you read his letters you'll see what an extremely complex character he really was. There's his extraordinary little painting of a baby, for example, which is in the museum in Amsterdam – it has all the essence and horror of a newborn child, its awful little bracelet and its horrible look. People think of Van Gogh mainly as a landscape painter, but he was also a marvellous painter of portraits and self-portraits.

You've always done a lot of self-portraits yourself, haven't you?

Generally I only do a self-portrait because I haven't got another subject around at the time, not because I'm interested in my own appearance – though of course one does know something about the contours of one's own face, from seeing it every day in the mirror. I also work from photographs, in fact, I often go to those booths where one takes passport photos, just to see how they'll turn out; but all photographs distort enormously, which most people never seem to realise. Anyway, I mainly do self-portraits when I haven't got anyone else to paint.

Do you think Rembrandt did self-portraits for the same reason?

I've no idea why he did them, although I certainly think that his self-portraits, from his youth to his old age, are among his most remarkable paintings.

And you're not conscious at all of making a kind of record of your inner feelings through your own self-portraits?

Not at all. You see, I don't think one knows what one's inner feelings are. I mean, you know what they are when you are very fond of somebody, for instance, but it's not in the least enlightening about your own character. It's true that when one thinks of Rembrandt's self-portraits, from the very early ones to the later ones, one can read into them an extraordinary graph of his life, but whether he meant it in that way one doesn't know.

One of the great problems of painting is how you can make a portrait that isn't just a photographic illustration of somebody. If you think of the great portraits of Rembrandt, they seem to be marvellous images – there's one in the National Gallery of an old woman called Maria Tripp; you don't so much think about her as of the extraordinary image that Rembrandt made. When you see her head on top of the ruff, it almost looks like one of those African heads that were boiled down, the image is concentrated so intensely. Whether it had anything to do with her character, as well as with his extraordinary ability, I don't know.

Tell me a bit about how you work, how you organise your day.
I get up in the morning and start painting, and just hope that something will come about, you know. I get up early, as soon as there's light. A lot of painters prefer working by night, and I used to years ago, but now I much prefer working by day. I generally work for five or six hours and then I stop – unless it happens to be going very well.

Do you start work with a feeling of excitement?
No, I don't. I think it's awful to be confronted with a ghastly blank canvas. I have a generalised idea of what I want to do, but I really don't know how to do it and I don't know what's going to come. I only enjoy it when it begins to work, when the possibilities of developing the image come about.

And what about when you stop painting? I believe you do quite a lot of gambling, for instance.
Yes, I often gamble in the evenings. It excites me up to a point and it's also a way of passing the time. It can become a drug, an obsession, but it isn't really in my case. I was brought up in an atmosphere of horse-racing and gambling from a very early age, and I think it probably comes from there.

Do you mind losing money?
Naturally I prefer to win but I'm a stupid gambler, and if I've got the money I don't regret it terribly if I lose it. After all, nearly all gamblers are losers.

What sort of people have your friends tended to be?
I naturally like people, as we all do, who've got reasonably

good looks; and if they're not struggling to earn money all the time, that's always a help. I used to prefer the company of crooks – or villains, as they like to call themselves. In a curious way – although I've had various things stolen from me – I find them less boring than most people.

Do you think spending so much of your childhood in Ireland has had a lasting influence on your character and outlook?
I think it must have had an influence on one's character. I'm not Irish, unfortunately – both my mother and father were English – but I'm very attached to Ireland. I like the people and I particularly like their natural gift for making sentences, their vivid conversation. You can see it in so many of their great writers – Yeats, Joyce, Wilde.

I know that literature means a great deal to you, that you read a lot of poetry. Does it give you ideas for painting?
Very much so. In an odd way, poems often create stronger images for me than things I've seen. Yeats had an enormous effect on me, and the early Eliot poems. Just now I'm thinking of starting a triptych suggested by the *Agamemnon*. Unfortunately I can't read Greek, but even in translation – I've read three or four different ones – you can see how terribly powerful Aeschylus is. There's the wonderful imagery, and even if it seems exaggerated, in an odd way it says something very powerful and very fundamental about existence.

I know this is a delicate question, but what effect do you think being homosexual has had on your painting?
I suppose it's made this difference: that when I paint the human body I tend to paint men rather than women. But the whole business of homosexuality is so complex; I don't think one has even begun to understand it. But then what does one understand about the emotions?

Has it made you unhappy?
No, it has never made me at all unhappy. I suppose in some ways it's a misfortune or limiting to be a homosexual, but I can't say that I've ever regretted it myself. It certainly made my parents very unhappy and upset when they realised – which they did when I was very young – that I had that tendency, or drive; but the morality of that time was so different from what it is now. It was considered outrageous to be a homosexual in those days, but then of course they didn't think historically about the thing at all.

Talking of history, has it ever made any difference to you that you're called Francis Bacon?
My father was actually descended from the family to which the Elizabethan Francis Bacon belonged, and they've always gone on calling one of the children Francis, and I happened to be the one. It's an unfortunate name to have, because he was such a very remarkable man, but I've never thought much about it or bothered to go into the details of my ancestry. Strangely enough, the original Francis Bacon was homosexual too.

Do you take much interest in politics?
I can't say that I have any strong feeling about which government is in power. Of course we've been lucky in this country, though I don't know how long it can go on for, in that we've had comparative freedom; and I think all one can ask for is as much freedom as one can reasonably have. I really don't care whether it's Conservative or Labour who's in, but one hopes not to have to live under a totalitarian regime – at least, I do.

And you've never wanted to express a political theme or message in your work?
No, because I've no message to give. When I look at my

paintings, I don't know what they are really about. But then in general when one thinks of works of art of the past one either doesn't know what they mean or the meaning they once had no longer matters in the way it did.

For instance, to me one of the great images of the world is the Sphinx, but I've no idea what the Sphinx is or represents. I know originally it was probably some kind of religious symbol, but to me its beauty is in the image – and the same is just as true of paintings of the Crucifixion.

Do you regret that you haven't got a religion or a tradition to work in, some belief that you can celebrate in your painting?
In a way I do. But if you think of somebody like Monet, he painted in celebration of beauty, the beauty of his garden and his water-lilies. I can't say that I paint in that way myself, but I think it is marvellous to have a subject that one is obsessed by.

Has becoming very well known as an artist made much difference to you?
Well, my pictures still only sell with great difficulty. They're not at all liked and not at all popular, but every so often somebody buys them. And if I have become better known, I certainly don't think it has made the slightest difference to me as a painter.

HAROLD PINTER
1980

Harold Pinter was in high spirits when I interviewed him shortly before his 50th birthday – and with good reason. He was finally free, after complicated divorce proceedings, to marry Lady Antonia Fraser. Theirs had been the most glamorous and dramatic public love affair of my generation, so sensational and unlikely that many people doubted it could possibly last. Apart from anything else, their backgrounds were totally incongruous: he came from a lower-middle-class Jewish family in the East End of London; she was born into the Anglo-Irish aristocracy and had married the son of a prominent Scottish lord. But the relationship had endured and they had now been living together for five years. Their wedding was planned to take place on his birthday. It was as though Anthony and Cleopatra, *or* Anna Karenina, *had been rewritten with happy endings.*

Our interview took place in the mews cottage where he worked; it was part of the house he and Antonia Fraser shared. Pinter was dressed in his customary black. Though we met in mid-afternoon, he immediately opened a bottle of white wine and continued to drink throughout our interview (as did I), becoming gradually more merry and loquacious. As for long pauses, there were none.

MIRIAM GROSS: Did you go to the theatre much, or at all, when you were a child? When did you first go?
HAROLD PINTER: At about the age of 15. The first thing I saw was Wolfit's company – *King Lear*, *Macbeth*. We were taken by my English master, who was a very remarkable man. He died last year; a great shock, actually. We'd remained close friends. The theatre meant a lot to him and he took a few of us to see Wolfit, and that left a great impression. *Lear* particularly, which I saw six times. I couldn't stop seeing it.

I know you acted Macbeth at school, but did you do Lear as well?
No, no. I acted Macbeth and then Romeo in productions by this particular master. But many years later I did actually act

in Wolfit's Lear. I was one of his knights.

Was acting your main interest at school?
No, not at all. Literature was my main interest, poetry – and sport, and girls. Those were the three things.

Did you start writing poetry yourself at about that time?
Yes, at about thirteen. Before that I wrote stories. And then I was very excited by the discoveries that one makes. I discovered and read Joyce very early on, and Eliot and Dostoevsky, Hemingway and Sartre, etcetera, etcetera. I had a pretty vigorous time with them all. I used to discuss them at great length with my friends.

And what about girls? Did you have much chance of meeting them, or did you have a very segregated English school life?
Not in the least. I went to a grammar school in Hackney – a pretty good school – and I used to go with my friends to a boys' and girls' club. We played ping-pong and eyed the girls.

Did you fall for them and develop crushes and so on?
Not them. When you say them, plural, that's not the case. I did have a pretty strong association with a girl in my early teens. But anyway, it was all rather different then. There was this dark world of sex which took place in mists and rain, in alleys and on park benches under trees. I remember it with a very special fondness; I hope for the sake of the young that it still exists somewhere. But the thing that really obsessed me was literature.

And was it literature, poetry, which led you on to drama?
No, I didn't think very much about the theatre then. I didn't read plays, apart from Shakespeare and some of

the Jacobeans. In fact, apart from Shakespeare, I can't remember the first time I saw an ordinary play. It must have been much later on.

I did go to RADA for a couple of terms, but I didn't get on very well there. I was quite out of my depth, really, with what I took to be the general sophistication, the knowingness about the place. I was pretty lost. The girl I mentioned just now was also at RADA, but in a higher class, and I'd lost her too.

So what did you do, just leave?
I didn't quite just leave. Although I was unhappy there, I still had my own kind of stability. I actually faked a nervous breakdown – in order to keep the grant, you see.

How does one do that?
One trains oneself to become extremely white in the face. Then you have to speak in a very low voice, hardly heard, and walk very slowly, and be on the verge of tears. All this worked extremely well.

Did you let any of your friends in on this?
I did, but my friends didn't know precisely when I was going to take the final step. And there was one quite extraordinary coincidence. It so happened that on the very day I was to have my last interview with the principal of RADA, I was standing in the lobby, and two of my friends suddenly came in through the front door of the place and said, 'Hello, Harold, coming to Lord's?' And I whispered, 'In five minutes – I'll meet you round the corner,' and then I went in and spoke in my low voice, on the verge of tears, and everything went perfectly well.

This interview was to establish that you were a broken man?

Yes, and the principal patted me on the back – he was a very nice man; I'm sorry I deceived him – and wished me well, and then I had leave of absence, you see. I walked very slowly out of RADA, very slowly down Gower Street, round the corner into Store Street – lovely day, by the way – and there were my friends. I ran towards them and shouted 'I'm free' and we jumped on a bus and went to Lord's – it was one of the happiest days of my life.

What about your parents, did they think you were still at RADA?

That's right, I got up at the same time every morning and left the house. This went on for some months, and I simply wandered about London. Cups of tea, and libraries, cricket, and I had just enough money to keep me going. When I got home I used to make up stories about what plays I was acting in, and so on.

Did you feel at all guilty towards your parents?

I was concerned about them, yes, but I had no alternative as I saw it. And I had a rather fruitful few months, mooching about.

It wasn't a kind of George Orwell down-and-out existence? Did you meet tramps and the kind of people that you put into your plays?

No, I wasn't storing anything away. I wasn't thinking in that way at all. I was also a conscientious objector at the time, which rather complicated things. I spent half the time waiting for trials and tribunals.

Why exactly were you a conscientious objector?

I've always had a deeply embedded suspicion of political structures, of governments and the way people are used by them. I was determined not to be used in that way. I was quite prepared to go to prison – I took my toothbrush along when I went to court, I was quite ready – and I was fortunate to be fined instead. I had two trials and was fined twice. My father paid the fines; my parents regretted the whole thing enormously, but they stood by me.

Would you have been a conscientious objector in, say, 1939?

No, certainly not. The feelings I had about National Service in 1948 wouldn't have applied in the war. I felt very strongly about the war. And still do, if you see what I mean. After all, I wasn't a child by the time it ended; though I was when it began.

I was evacuated – at the age of nine – and that left a deep mark on me, as I think it did on all children who were evacuated. To be suddenly scooped out of one's home and to find oneself hundreds of miles away – as I did, in Cornwall – was very strange. I was very lonely there, pretty miserable, although it was also very, very beautiful and that remained with me too. But it was a desolate beauty; because I myself was desolate.

And how did you get back into acting, after you'd left RADA?

Well, actually I did go to another drama school for about a year, the Central School, and that was OK. I had a certain ability of a limited kind as an actor, and I couldn't see any other way of earning a living; I couldn't face the idea of going into an office.

After the Central I did some things on radio, and then I went to Ireland for two or three years to work with Anew McMaster, the last of the great actor-managers. He was a wonderful man. It was great work, but very hard. We did seven plays a week, mostly Shakespeare, and we moved about a lot.

Were you still writing through all this time?

Oh yes, I was writing quite a lot, a lot of poetry. The first poems of mine that were published were in *Poetry London* in 1950, when I was twenty. They accepted two of my poems and I was immensely pleased. But when I got the magazine and opened it I saw that they'd actually mixed the two poems together – two verses of one were followed by two verses of the other, and vice versa. The poems were pretty obscure at the best of times, but this made them quite incomprehensible. Naturally I was very upset, but later on they reprinted them the right way round.

When did you first have the idea of writing a play?

A friend of mine, Henry Woolf, who was studying drama at Bristol University wanted to put on a play and asked me if I'd write one. I said no, absolutely not, I'd never written a play. Then I said, well, I do have an idea, in fact. He said, right, write it and I'll do it, and I said, well, I'll see. A couple of weeks later he rang up and said, where's the play? I said, don't be ridiculous, it will take me six months at least to write it. He said, it can't take six months because I have to go into rehearsal next week. I said, well, forget it. And then I wrote the play in three days. That was *The Room* and he did it, and that was that.

It's rather surprising, don't you think, that you hadn't thought of writing plays before, since so many of your themes seem to lend themselves much more to drama than to poetry – conflict, people struggling for dominance or waging a war of nerves. And there's a lot of violence in them. Do you tend to see life in these terms?

I never think about what I think about life. I myself prefer a quiet life. But that isn't quite what we are faced with, is it, either outside ourselves or within ourselves? While we're talking now, for example, people are locked up in prisons all over the place, being tortured in one way or another. I'm quite raddled with these kinds of images, with the sense that these things are ever-present. I have plenty of violence within me, and from a child I've lived in a world in which there has been more and more violence of one sort or another. It's as simple as that, I think.

For example, after the war – this is something which very few people are aware of now – there was a considerable amount of Fascist activity in the East End of London. In 1945, after the war. In the streets round a Jewish club I used to go to, and around the Ridley Road market – there was a big fascist stronghold there – we used to bump into quite a few of the boys, you know, and we had a number of set-tos. It was really quite ugly. They used to beat up old Jews in the Dalston Junction area.

In many respects it was a perfectly lively, quite vigorous community down there, but when the night fell you never knew what you were going to meet. I've never understood how the Fascists were given that kind of leeway.

Another feature of your plays is that so many of the characters seem to have guilty pasts; there's a sort of something-nasty-in the-woodshed feeling about them.
Well, I don't think there can be anyone alive who doesn't carry around a load of junk in his head which is his past life, and other people's lives. When one looks back, one can hardly be complacent about anything that has happened in one's life. I suppose the characters in these plays are heightened examples of people walking around with this load, this burden of things ill done, badly done.

I know you're a great admirer of Proust – you've written a screenplay based on *A la Recherche* – and he of course was a writer obsessed with the past. But in many ways you seem complete opposites. Proust is tremendously

analytical; he constantly explains characters and their motives, while in your plays there are very few explanations; lots of questions are left unanswered.

Well, I wouldn't talk about Proust and myself in the same breath, but you obviously don't have to be the same kind of animal as the person you admire. Just because I don't go in for that kind of analysis in my own writing doesn't mean that I can't appreciate it in somebody else's work, particularly when it's Proust. And there are so many layers in Proust apart from the analysis – his marvellously precise visual sense, for example, which is quite staggering if you read him very carefully. Certainly I've never had a year like the one I spent working on *A la Recherche*.

The thing about Proust is, finally, the weight of the whole damn thing and its unerring accuracy – it moves one deeply. In a way that Joyce, for instance, doesn't, although Joyce has always been my boy, from the word go. But Joyce is really much more of a comic writer, in my view.

One of the great themes in Proust, and in literature generally, is romantic or obsessive love. I may be wrong, but there doesn't seem to be much love of that kind in your plays.

I think I'll put on my dark glasses for this one. I think there's a good deal of love about in some of my plays. But love can very easily go down the wrong path and be distorted as a result of frustration in all kinds of different ways. In *The Homecoming*, for example, the violence of the family towards their son when he comes back from America, using his wife to embody their own rage and spleen or whatever, comes about because they don't know where to put their love. I think there's a great deal of love in that play but they simply don't know what to do with it.

There's a lot of courtesy and formality in your plays as

well as aggression. Is courtesy important to you?
Yes, I do think courtesy is worth paying attention to. As long as it's genuine, not the hollow kind one bumps into all along the line. But spontaneity is the thing, isn't it? Mind you, not the kind of spontaneity that leads Americans to call you by your first name without knowing you. They can throw that kind of spontaneity down the drain as far as I'm concerned.

Today, for example, a fellow phoned me out of the blue; he didn't actually call me Harold, but he almost did. He said he'd written me a letter some time ago, and had I got it? I remained quite silent and he stuttered on to say that it was about a symposium in Ohio in 1982 or something, which he was trying to get together, and how much he'd like me to take part, etcetera, etcetera, etcetera. Eventually I said, 'How did you get my telephone number? Who gave you my telephone number?'

I really do resent this kind of intrusion.

What do you feel about the fact that you are going to be 50 this week?
I feel rather good about it. I'm quite fit. I'm finding life rather a lively business in my 50th year.

Do you think one changes very much as one gets older – becomes less intense, for instance?
I damn well hope I'm less intense now than I was when I was young. But I don't think one's feelings become any less strong, certainly not. In many ways quite the contrary. They're sharpened, heightened as one grows older; one's sight becomes rather longer, which also means that you can spot a dud a mile off, something that's a posture rather than a true state of affairs.

Do you feel at all what traditionally people are supposed

to feel, that you're becoming more conservative, that the country is going to the dogs, and so on?

I certainly have strong feelings about values and standards. I think there is less appreciation of quality; things have become less serious – for obvious reasons, I would have thought. The world's in such a state of panic, so anxious to get through the day without one of those lovely missiles from Norfolk exploding. I think there's a great deal of nuclear panic about, without people recognising it or referring to it, and this dictates many attitudes – the quick buck, the quick poem, the quick song, the quick whatever you like. And this means that it's 'pop' which has come to dominate everything.

You've mentioned cricket more than once. Why does it appeal to you so much?

I tend to believe that cricket is the greatest thing that God ever created on earth.

Greater than sex, for example?

Certainly greater than sex, although sex isn't too bad either. But everyone knows which comes first when it's a question of cricket or sex – all discerning people recognise that. Anyway, don't forget one doesn't have to do two things at the same time. You can either have sex before cricket or after cricket – the fundamental fact is that cricket must be there at the centre of things. To put my cards on the table, I must also say that cricket means England to me.

In what particular way?

Well, the first thing is that you play cricket on grass, and I know there are grasses all over the world, but it's not like English grass, you know.

No, I want to correct this: it doesn't finally matter about

the grass or the horses looking over the hedge or the white clouds in the summer sky and all that. You can also play cricket in pouring rain; well, not pouring rain but terrible drizzle, on an awful ground with a miserable bar (the bar of course is one of the points of cricket) with bloody awful beer and terrible sandwiches, and, as I say, pissing rain which you still have to play in because it isn't pissing quite enough – in other words, a context which is quite displeasing; but the fact remains that whatever the context the overall activity is still a thing of beauty and the people taking part in it, believe it or not, are in a certain sense transformed by it.

Although it's often full of bad humour and irritations and selfishness, I do think – and this is a very nineteenth-century view of it all – that the game of cricket is good for the moral fibre and soul of the people engaged in it.

To get back to your plays, do you enjoy seeing them performed?

On the whole, yes. But what I find rather interesting is that my last three full-length plays have hardly been performed at all in this country, outside London. My last play, *Betrayal*, for instance, has been produced all over the world in the past year – there have been 23 separate productions in West Germany alone – but so far only one English provincial theatre has put it on – the Haymarket Theatre, Leicester, where it's running at the moment.

You've written quite a number of screenplays, haven't you?

Yes, I enjoy doing them, particularly the last one I did, *The French Lieutenant's Woman*: it was a very difficult task but totally absorbing. I've seen a good deal of the shooting and I really think it's going to be quite a film.

Do you go to the cinema much yourself?

When I was young a great deal of my life was spent at the cinema, but nowadays I almost never go. One of the reasons I don't go is that I find it difficult to sit among groups of people. I find it difficult to concentrate – the whispering, the chatting, the eating of the popcorn.

The real sin embedded in the cinema system is the packets in which they keep their chocolates and their popcorn. The poor bastards who have spent so much time trying to get it right up there on the screen – there's an outrage inflicted on them by the splitting, the ripping of these packages. I feel I'm going to burst a blood vessel and you can't keep saying 'Shut up, shut up' all the time. People don't know what you're talking about.

The last time I went to our local cinema to see a film I very much wanted to see, *Interiors*, I found it quite intolerable – the smell and the splitting of bloody popcorn all over the place – and I left. So I'm becoming a crusty old man after all.

One gets the impression that you are a rather solitary individual. Do you see yourself in that way?
No. I don't think so. Antonia Fraser and I have lived together very happily for five years and are about to marry. And I have a good many friends; I also spend a great deal of my life with actors, and enjoy their company very much.

You don't find them narcissistic, vain and so on?
Not at all. I think the image of actors as children, narcissistic and vain, is quite inaccurate. They're very hard-working people, people with considerable imagination and intelligence, on the whole. As a body of people I respect actors more than I respect any other body of people. I can't think of any other body. Oh yes, apart from cricketers.

ANTHONY POWELL
1985

My interview with Anthony Powell is rather a painful memory. It started off happily enough. Powell greeted me at the front door of his beautiful house in Somerset with the words 'I've cooked you one of my curry lunches'. He was wearing a stripy cook's apron which, however, did not detract from his handsome, dignified appearance. It has often been said of him that his manner and bearing were more those of a military than of a literary man, and this certainly seemed true to me. At the same time I knew that he was an exceptionally shrewd and penetrating observer of human behaviour and I couldn't help wondering – dreading – what he might say about me to his wife Violet after I had left. She had presided at our lunch, which took place in their formal dining room. The curry was excellent.

During the interview Powell was less reserved and more expansive than I had expected, so I was very pleased with the way it had gone. When I got home I turned on the tape-recorder. There was nothing on it – except a continuous whirring sound. What a disaster. I must somehow have failed to switch it on properly. What to do? I couldn't possibly remember most of what Powell had said and, anyway, I strongly believe in reproducing an interviewee's exact words and turns of phrase. My deadline – Powell's 80th birthday – was looming. I finally braced myself to phone the poor man and explain what had happened. Would it be at all possible to come again? For a much shorter time? Powell very kindly agreed. But on my second visit his manner was unmistakeably – and wholly justifiably – cool. And there was no curry lunch.

MIRIAM GROSS: Ever since 'The Music of Time' started appearing, people have speculated on how far the characters in it have real-life originals. To what extent did you in fact portray people you knew?
ANTHONY POWELL: It's often thought that the most definite kind of individuals will make the best characters in novels, but it's not at all like that. It's people whose personalities are somewhat unrealised who make you think about them and then gradually develop them into figures in novels. Definite characters from real life hardly ever work in novels. A good example is in *The Possessed*, a novel I tremendously admire, where Dostoevsky put in Turgenev as one of the characters, and it simply doesn't work.

People who don't themselves write novels always seem to think that the only way to do it is to think of somebody and then draw some kind of picture of them, but this is miles from what really happens. It's very difficult to say what you do in novels. I simply don't know how it works. What I do know is that in my own novels I don't like to go in for pure invention – I don't like describing characteristics or incidents which in my own mind, at least, I can't attribute to someone I know or something that has happened to me.

If someone's good for being a character, he's probably good for being half a dozen characters. Or it can work the other way. I've just been re-reading Painter's marvellous life of Proust, and he sometimes produces about a dozen people who have gone into making just one of Proust's characters.

There are obviously many parallels with Proust in your own work. To what extent did you have him in mind when you started 'The Music of Time'?
I think it's impossible for anybody writing a serious novel since the 1920s not to be influenced by Proust in one way or another. I've always been a tremendous admirer, and there's no doubt I've learnt a lot from him. But I don't think I'm at

all the same sort of person, and of course he was enormously interested in himself, in his own psychology, while I'm not – I'm much more interested in other people's.

Your narrator may not go in for Proustian self-examination, but one nevertheless gets to know him very well by the end of the novel.
Well, everyone in a sense is interested in themselves, and it is a whole area in which I think it's very difficult to speak honestly. From my earliest childhood I've always been fascinated by other people and how they behave and what they do, and I like to see myself in relation to them. I'm not suggesting that's any less egotistical than being interested in yourself in a straightforward way. But when you're writing a book there are technical considerations about how to deal with yourself which may have a very important bearing on everything else in it. To mention Proust again, he is sometimes attacked for not making his narrator a homosexual or half-Jewish, both of which he was himself, but it seems to me that if he had he would have risked writing a homosexual novel or a Jewish novel, which might have been very interesting but was not in fact the novel he wanted to write.

Do you think that in order to create characters a novelist has to some extent to have similar feelings to theirs?
Yes. There is no doubt that in a sense you are everybody in your book. You have to imagine them, and so a small part of you is them, and I think that's an extremely important part of writing a novel. Writing novels is such a curious business – the more I do it, the less I know how it's done. Novelists live with all these images in their minds all the time, and very few critics know what that's like. It has often seemed to me that Barbara Cartland and Proust have more in common with each other than either of them has with Dr Leavis.

Do you ever find that these images you carry around get confused with reality?
In an odd way, they do. In fact, I sometimes have difficulty in remembering exactly what happened to me and what was invented in the novel. It's rather like a dream – you know you're in one place, although in fact it looks like another. In the same way one knows one has put certain things in a novel because in a sense they're true, though they didn't exactly happen that way.

One of the characters in your novel says: 'Human beings aren't subtle enough to play their part. That's where art comes in.' Is that your own view?
I think that people often don't realise how moving or how dramatic something they say is, or if you like, how extraordinarily generous or evil their gestures can be. Fiction can bring all that into perspective. I think the novel has quite extraordinary powers in that respect.

In all your work it seems to me you've been fairly right-wing. You associate the Left with opportunism and hypocrisy and foolishness. Is that a fair impression?
Well, I've never been very political, but I didn't feel at all drawn to the conventional Leftism of the 1930s. In those days the only thing you were allowed to be was a kind of parlour communist. Everybody was saying what a gallant chap Stalin was and how splendid Russia was and so on, which was very unsympathetic to me then, and looking back it's even more unsympathetic to me now. I think a lot of our troubles now originate in the 1920s or 30s.

Did you feel really isolated, or did you have some friends who shared your views?
I did have friends who weren't particularly political. Constant Lambert, for instance – I remember him saying that Auden's

poems were like reading a lot of back numbers of the *New Statesman*. But there was a moment at the beginning of the 1930s when anybody who didn't belong to the Left was totally swept off the book pages.

Three of the volumes of 'The Music of Time' are about the Second World War, and they seem to me perhaps the most powerful part of the work. Did the war have as deep an impact on you as this suggests? Did it change you a great deal?

Oh, I think enormously. You were shunted about physically and you met people who you couldn't possibly have met otherwise. I found myself in a Welsh battalion in which nearly all the men were miners and nearly all the officers had worked in banks. I had had absolutely no training for seventeen years, since I'd been in the Training Corps at school, and suddenly one had to take 50 Welsh miners and show them how to attack a hill or something like that. Later I was in the War Office and had to deal with various allies – Poles, Czechs, Belgians, French – and one met some strange people in that way. It was the time of my life when I would, I suppose, have been most prolific as a novelist, between the ages of 34 and 40. But everything was dammed up and in abeyance, and you came out after six years with a different perspective, with a lot of things you wanted to write about instead of having to write about nothing in particular. For me it couldn't have worked out better.

How would you compare your attitude to the war in your books with Evelyn Waugh's?

I don't know about the war, but our attitudes to the army were bound to be rather different. My father was a professional soldier and so were quite a lot of my relations, and I was brought up with the idea that being in the army was an absolutely normal profession for a man to have. Until I was about fourteen I always thought I would go into the army myself, so that when the war came, joining the army wasn't anything like as strange to me as it was to many people. Evelyn Waugh, when he wrote about aspects of army life which he didn't experience himself, was often hopelessly ill at ease. Indeed, he inscribed one of his books to me with an apologetic note for the mistakes in it –there are certain technicalities he never really knew about. I have no doubt that he was exceedingly brave, and there was never any question of his not wanting to be in the army – but he didn't quite get the hang of it in the way one does if one has had it all around from one's earliest days.

You say somewhere that marriage is quite different from any other relationship, and it may take 20 or 30 years to test the implications of a given partner.
Yes, I think that marriage for some reason is a totally different relationship from just cohabiting with somebody, but why that should be – it's just one of the mysteries of life, I think. Everybody develops new characteristics as time goes on.

Do you think there's something secret or secretive about all marriages which makes them different from other relationships?
Well, I think there's certainly something secret about all marriages and indeed about life in general. The whole of life is secret. The more you try to describe certain things, the further you may get from what they're really like. For example, sexual relations – the more explicit you are, the further from reality you may be.

Are you at all shocked by the explicitness and permissiveness of recent years?
I'm not shocked by it; I think it's perfectly all right, provided people realise that it's going to land them in an awful lot of

trouble. Because all sex life sooner or later lands you in what, for want of a better word, I would call trouble.

It is often said that in England, in contrast to other countries – France, for instance – writers are not sufficiently honoured. Do you feel that there has been any lack of celebration of yourself?
Not in the least. Indeed, I think that such celebration of literary men as there is in this country is probably rather an embarrassment. The French thing has got to be seen against the whole background of French life.

And then there's the way authors are feted in America.
Yes, apparently you're treated like a film star. I can't imagine anything I would enjoy less.

You're obviously in favour of English understatement.
Well, it has always seemed to me that putting things into words makes much more difference than people think. There are so many things in life that are altered once you've said them. Some people complained about my memoirs that 'he doesn't really tell us anything about himself,' but there's quite a difference between somebody knowing that you had an affair with such-and-such a girl, for instance, and your saying 'I had an affair with such-and-such a girl.' It could be a good thing or a bad thing, but it's not the same thing.

In 'The Music of Time' there's quite a lot about the seven deadly sins, especially about a tapestry depicting them. Do you think there's one of them you're particularly prone to?
Let me think – they all attract me so much. Lust, obviously. Anger, obviously. Avarice, not so much, though it has its attractive moments. Pride, yes. Sloth – I'm not exactly given to sloth, more to accidie, the feeling that nothing's worth

doing. I'm absolutely overcome by that most of the time. Envy – I think I'm free of envy: I suffer from it as little as anybody reasonably could. But I think I could put up quite a good game at any of them.

The book is going to be adapted for television by Ken Taylor, who also did *The Jewel in the Crown*. Did you watch it?
I didn't the first time round because I get exceedingly irritated by the anti-Britishness of so many films about India. We did a frightfully good job in India, as anyone who goes there can see for themselves. But I'm watching it now, and I think it's extremely good.

Can you tell me some recent writers that you've admired, and also some that you think are overrated?
I like Kingsley Amis's novels and I like V.S. Naipaul, and recently I've rather liked A.N. Wilson. But I don't think it's part of the job of a novelist to appear, you know, as a kind of general critic of other novelists. And one of the things that one never realises when one is young is how difficult it is to keep up with what young people are doing unless you're in some job which keeps you in touch; because what you're mainly doing is keeping up with your own generation. As for writers I don't like, I don't want to talk about them; I don't see any need for it – I think minding your own business is a very good thing.

Are you worried about giving offence?
No, not a bit if it's necessary, but I don't want to go out of my way to give offence.

As one can see from your memoirs, you're very interested in genealogy. What particularly attracts you to it?
Yes, I've always been extremely interested in it. It's something

that absolutely enrages people, for some reason; I never know why.

I suppose it's thought to be connected with snobbery.
I suppose it is, but in fact, it's quite the reverse. It teaches you how tremendously fluid classes in England are. And it's about people, of course. And then it's got a cross-word puzzle side to it – once you're interested in it, it becomes very exciting finding things out and slotting them in, rather like playing patience.

Do you have any special feelings about being 80?
Being 80 is a matter of extraordinarily little interest to me. One just feels exactly as one did, except rather less spry, with less good ideas, slower and so on.

What age would you ideally like to be?
I think one's forties are really the pleasantest time. That's the age I would choose to be if I had a kind of cruising speed to remain at. I certainly don't want to be young again. I can't think of anything more awful.

Acknowledgements

I am very grateful to Fiona Maddocks, Edward Mirzoeff, Leina Schiffrin and especially to my husband, Geoffrey Owen, for their encouragement and editorial advice.